M000189828

Are your kids approaching or already in their tween or teen years? Do you worry about them making the best choices for their lives both now and in the future in this ever- changing world? Whether you're a mother with a career or a career mom, *Mom's Don't Quit!* is a highly practical guide that will help you and your children survive and thrive during these challenging years.

Dr. Yanina is highly knowledgeable and provides sound advice for conscientious mothers (and fathers) who not only want to raise healthy individuals that will contribute to our world but want to nurture and sustain strong relationships with their children while maintaining their own well-being in the process.

Regina Campbell, M.A., retired school
psychologist and mother of two sons

If you have been experiencing the parenting pains that go along with raising teens/tweens, then this book is for you! Not only is Dr. Yanina knowledgeable about the struggles of teens and tweens, but also has experience raising her own. In her book, she discusses how to become a better parent while simultaneously building confidence and self-love within your teen/tween. She gives practical suggestions for connecting and communicating with your child. Further, she gives mothers emotional wellness strategies, emphasizing that if you are an emotionally well parent, you will be better equipped to deal with and tune into the challenging developmental stages of your child. I love that Dr. Yanina's book is accompanied by a workbook that provides guidance through a dialogue and thoughtful discussions. Her guidance will help you parent your teen/tween through a compassionate and structured approach.

Amy M. Cramer, PhD, mother of two young children

Dr. Yanina's book addresses the age-old issue of maintaining healthy relationships with our children during critical times in their physical and emotional development. Her approach is sincere and relatable as she references real life problems, obstacles, and concerns of the ever-changing family dynamics during a period in a child's life when he/she begins to question everything.

Dr. Yanina explains how understanding and empathy will help mothers connect to their own child's struggles. She offers very practical, relatable, and usable techniques as examples in her book. Most unique is that the book includes two chapters on one's own wellness, which is not only a way to maintain one's own emotional well-being, but also to model healthy wellness to our children. In an age of conflicting messages and nonstop media and social media influences, Dr. Yanina offers parents the opportunity to enrich the lives of future generations in this guide to health and well-being.

Ruth Crnkovich, M.A., mother of twin sons

In her book, *Mom's Don't Quit!,* Dr. Yanina addresses critical developmental and mental health concerns potentially affecting the relationship between mothers and their tween and teen children. An expert in her field, Dr. Yanina has in-depth knowledge and invaluable resources for guiding mothers to identify and resolve many of the difficulties they will encounter assisting their children transition from childhood to adolescence.

Dr. Yanina exhorts mothers to stay connected with their tween and teen, emphasizing the importance of strengthening and repairing broken ties. She suggests that mothers help their adolescent children regulate their nascent sense of independence, self-image and relationships with peers through empathic and age appropriate discipline. These are noteworthy recommendations since relationships with peers and psychological separation and individuation from parents are major developmental milestones for adolescents.

Importantly, Dr. Yanina encourages mothers to take care of themselves by attending to their own emotional struggles and reflecting on how these factors may be interfering with optimal parenting. I commend Dr. Yanina for launching such an important book and for her dedication to helping mothers traverse the challenges of parenthood.

Lilia Smith, PhD Clinical psychologist in private practice in Coral Gables, Florida, previously clinical supervisor at the Children Psychiatric Center in Miami Florida.

Moms Don't Quit!

How to Influence, Empower, and Stay Connected with Your Tween or Teen in a Noisy World

A. Yanina Gomez, PhD

Published by Author Academy Elite
P.O. Box 43, Powell, OH 43035

www.AuthorAcademicElite.com

Paperback ISBN: 978-1-64085-208-2

Hardcover ISBN: 978-1-64085-210-5

Ebook ISBN: 978-1-64085-209-9

Library of Congress Control Number: 2018933830

This book is dedicated to my amazing husband Sergio for always bringing out the best in me and his unlimited support, my son Alec for coming home from school one day and frantically telling me that I've got to write a book for moms of tweens and teens, my daughter Nyah for encouraging and cheering me up each time I completed a chapter, my parents for instilling excellence in me, and my siblings for believing in me.

I'm also grateful to my amazing inner-circle of friends, for their encouragement and support, and my Creator for enlightening me with the words I'm sharing with you in this book.

CONTENTS

PART THREE. PRIORITIZING MY OWN EMOTIONAL WELLNESS

FOREWORD

In this electronic age, tweens and teens are constantly bombarded by overwhelmingly conflicting messages coming from the media, internet, pop culture, fashion industry, and peer pressure. With advertisements featuring images of flawless bodies, perfect relationships, and unrealistic expectations everywhere they turn, tweens and teens lack direction becoming particularly vulnerable to experiencing issues with self-confidence, identity, relationships, and mental health.

Most moms agree that they want to raise healthy, confident, happy, and independent members of society. They'll also tell you that, as children enter the adolescent years, parenting and family life become more complicated. Some youngsters suddenly begin to distance themselves from their parents. More than ever, staying connected and strengthening the relationship between mom and child is essential to influence, guide, and make a greater impact in the lives of our youth.

As a mom of a tween daughter and a teen son, Dr. Yanina shares personal stories, what's working and what's not with her children. As a psychologist, she shares her experience with various parenting styles, family struggles, and providing supportive parenting, academic, and behavioral interventions. She also shares real-life examples, practical advice, and steps you can take right away to strengthen your relationship with your child and develop a healthier connection while teaching, empowering, and preparing them to succeed. Finally, she shares strategies to help you overcome inner-struggles and distractions that may be preventing you from being the mom you're meant to be.

As a wellness advocate, Dr. Yanina teaches moms the value of investing in their wellness so that they can adopt and model for their children a healthier mindful lifestyle. She believes when moms overcome their inner-struggles and insecurities they'll become the mother they're meant to be. Consequently, they'll make better decisions for their families and face hurdles in a more optimistic way.

As you read this book, you'll learn practical tips to help you stay connected and communicate more efficiently with your youngster in a way that makes an impact in their lives. You'll also learn effective ways to discipline and coach your child in a healthier way, better understand and support them during this critical developmental stage, and learn practical action steps to help your tween or teen overcome pressures, become more confident and independent. She dedicates the last two chapters of the book to help moms adopt healthier habits that lead to a mindful, intentional, and purposeful life. The bottom line is this—if we want our children to be confident, independent, honest, happy adults, we must be intentional about staying involved in their lives and guide them throughout this challenging season. This book will show you how.

Kary Oberbrunner, author of
Elixir Project and *Your Secret Name*
Igniting Souls
www.karyoberbrunner.com

INTRODUCTION
THE MISSING LINK

In today's noisy world, most tweens and teens are constantly bombarded by overwhelmingly conflicting messages from pop culture, internet, fashion industries, media, and their peers. With advertisements featuring images of flawless bodies, perfect relationships, and unrealistic expectations everywhere they turn, tweens and teens lack direction becoming particularly vulnerable to experiencing issues with self-confidence, identity, relationships, and mental health. Unfortunately, our kids aren't immune to these pressures, let alone ready to face them without being influenced one way or another.

The truth is, you have what it takes to influence, empower, and stay connected with your tween or teen despite the loud noises of this world. If our children are going to become confident, independent, honest, happy adults, as moms, we must be intentional about staying connected and involved in their lives so that we can guide them throughout this challenging season. If you're wondering how you can do this, you're reading the right book.

Before we get started and to get the most of this book, I encourage you to do four things:

1. Download and print the *Moms Don't Quit! Reflective Workbook* that accompanies this book. In this workbook, you'll find exercises to help you personalize the tips and strategies taught in this book chapter by chapter. It will also guide you through creating action steps to develop a stronger relationship with your child. The link to download this workbook is www.DrYaninaGomez.com/workbook.

2. Commit to investing in your personal growth, be truthful to yourself, and be willing to evaluate how you do parenting with an open mind.

3. Schedule "me-time" to read this book and complete the self-reflection exercises found on the Reflective Workbook.

4. Take the necessary steps to influence, empower, and stay connected with your tween or teen so you can become the mom you want to be.

From one mom to another, I know motherhood isn't easy. It feels like we're constantly riding a roller coaster of emotions. In the blink of an eye, we go from experiencing indescribable joy and pride, to quickly shifting into disappointment, anger, and frustration (sigh). Wouldn't it be nice if our children included a user manual at birth? Despite this overlook from the baby factory, you and I can raise awesome kids!

I'm very excited that you're taking the steps to becoming the best mom you can be. And, I am thankful to you for choosing me to ride along with you during this amazing journey. As you read this book, my goal is that you enjoy, learn, laugh, cry, reflect on what's working and what's not, gain more confidence, or perhaps affirm your parenting style. Most importantly, I encourage you to take the necessary steps to strengthen your relationship with your child. At the end of the day my dear reader, it all goes down to this—moms don't quit!

1

CONNECTING WITH MY TWEEN / TEEN AUTHENTICALLY

"Motherhood is a choice you make every day, to put someone else's happiness and well-being ahead of your own, to teach the hard lessons, to do the right thing even when you're not sure what is the right thing is . . . and to forgive yourself, over and over again, for doing everything wrong."

—Donna Ball

From the moment our children were born, they became the priority of our lives. After all, they were tiny people that relied on mom and dad for everything. From feeding, bathing, changing nasty diapers, cleaning up puke, wiping off boogers, to their never-ending appointments, my husband and I had to do everything for them. We not only took care of their basic needs, we also bombarded them with massive love including, but not limited to hugs, kisses, and big, loving squeezes. I was fully in-tune with everything and anything about my children.

When my daughter and son went to elementary school, I remained fully involved in their lives. I attended every Parent

Orientation Night and volunteered for classroom parties and fieldtrips as much as I could. I wanted to meet the person who was going to become the next influencer in their lives. I kept in touch with their teachers throughout the school year, often went online to check out their grades and assignments, and also made sure homework was done before bedtime. Of course, the massive kissing and hugging shebang was still going on. I wanted to be my children's greatest supporter and influencer.

Then middle school came for my son. I still attended Parent Orientation Nights and still do. But frankly, I suddenly began to let go without even noticing it. I wasn't communicating with his teachers as much, would rarely go online to check his grades, and no longer reminded him about homework.

I also cut down on kisses and hugs. I wanted to teach him responsibility and independence, however, in the process I was also disconnecting with him. That's when I realized that, regardless of the age of my tween, if I'm not intentional about staying connected with them, our relationship can potentially fade away. I want to teach them to be responsible and independent, but if I'm not careful, I may put our relationship at risk along the way.

We are born to be social people, and physical affection is a very important component in our development. Research has shown that adults who received affection and care from their parents, experience less depression and anxiety, are more sensitive toward others people's perspectives, and are more compassionate toward others[1].

Let's think about this for a second. How would you feel if you know you have someone who loves and supports you even when you show your true colors? Do you feel a sense of belonging, safety, confidence, and peace of mind?

The same is true for your tween or teen. When your daughter or son knows that you truly want to establish an authentic connection with them, they might not always tell you (or maybe they do!), but you're giving them an opportunity to

REGARDLESS OF HOW YOUR RELATIONSHIP IS WITH YOUR CHILD AT THIS MOMENT, WHETHER IT'S GOOD OR COMPLICATED, IT'S NEVER TOO LATE TO STRENGTHEN OR MEND IT.

experience these feelings. Regardless of how your relationship is with your child at this moment, whether it's good or complicated, it's never too late to strengthen or mend it.

I'm sure you want your tween or teen to experience a healthier adolescence and being connected with your child is the key. Having an authentic connection with your youngster is very important. Those who never experience this connection with their mom are at higher risk of experiencing physical conditions that pose a significant health risk such as high cholesterol, cardiovascular disease, and metabolic syndrome. As you see, being connected with your tween or teen is essential for a healthier development.

Now that you understand and agree with the value and importance of connecting with your tween or teen, let's do something about it. Maybe, you've been trying to get closer to your daughter or son and things are not going well. You feel that your tween or teen is keeping his distance and even avoiding you. You're probably feeling frustrated by failed attempts to connect and are almost ready to throw in the towel.

Please don't quit! If you stop trying, your tween or teen can mistakenly interpret it as uncaring indifference.

I can sense your frustration. You're probably sabotaging yourself, claiming that you're failing as a mom. Maybe mindset blocks like, "I'm not a good mom, my kids deserve a better mom than me, or I keep on messing up," are invading your mind and hurting your confidence.

There is a reason why you're reading this book. You are not failing as a mom. You want to influence, empower and stay connected with your tween or teen authentically. And you will! You've already taken the first step to becoming the mom you long to be.

hours. She's a very touchy-feely kind of girl. Our son is not the touchy-feely type.

When I was practicing as a psychologist, often times moms of tweens and teens would ask me: Where did my sweet, cute, lovely child go? One mom asked me once (be ready for this one!) "Do you think aliens use their (adolescents') bodies as a host?"

Although this is a funny question, most moms of tweens and tweens agree that their sweet, cute, lovely child has mutated into an indifferent emotionless creature once they arrive at adolescence. They feel disconnected with their child once she or he reaches this developmental stage. Although these feelings are more common than not, don't assume that your daughter or son no longer wants your affection. I made that mistake!

When my son was younger, he gave me hugs and kisses before leaving for school, when I picked him up from the after-school program, and before heading to bed. When he reached the age of twelve, like many tweens, he began to cut down his affection towards me, especially in public.

Without even noticing it, I was also showing less affection toward him until I caught myself and realized how wrong I was. Just because he wants to pretend to be cool doesn't mean that he doesn't appreciate his mother's affection.

I believe that, as long as you're alive, it's never too late to make adjustments and changes. So, I did. I changed course and pulled out of my sleeve a few old tricks that were not going to stain his reputation or invade his personal space. I respected that he was no longer a young child and that I had to go easy on the "hug and kiss shebang" when we were in public.

WHEN IN DOUBT, ASK.

We've been told that when in doubt, simply ask, right? That's exactly what I did. I asked my son if he prefers that I refrain from showing him affection in public. His answer really

TO AVOID
HEARTBREAKS AND
MISUNDERSTANDINGS
BETWEEN YOU AND YOUR
YOUNGSTER ABOUT HOW
TO SHOW AFFECTION,
I ENCOURAGE YOU TO
HAVE A CONVERSATION
WITH THEM.

impressed me. He said, "Mami (that's mom in Spanish), I don't mind you showing affection in public but I prefer that you go easy on me." Translation— don't overdo it. Kisses can wait until we get home and hugs are okay if the situation merits it. As much as possible, wait until we get home.

To avoid heartbreaks and misunderstandings between you and your youngster about how to show affection, I encourage you to have a conversation with them. Find a time when you and your child are in a good mood and willing to have a conversation. Don't start this conversation after coming home from work or in the middle of a busy day. Instead, try before heading to bed, on your way to or from after-school activities, or even chill together for a little while at a local coffeehouse.

Start by saying, "Chris, I know you're growing up and you know I love showing you how much I love you. Now that you're older, I want to know what makes you comfortable and uncomfortable."

Ask your tween or teen:

1. Are you okay with me showing you affection in private and in public?

2. What type of affection are you comfortable with in private and in public?

3. What type of affection are you uncomfortable with in private and in public?

Start the conversation, be willing to listen to what they have to say about this issue, and avoid becoming defensive.

Respect their individual comfort level, don't tease them, and don't take it personally.

Most importantly, never embarrass or mock your tween or teen in public. Each time you embarrass your child, you're breaking their trust in you. Keep in mind your child is experiencing drastic changes, many of them uncomfortable and hard to process.

Don't judge them. Instead, be patient, compassionate, and show understanding. Keep in mind that preferences might change as they go through different stages.

I've learned how to show affection to my son whether in private or in public. I took the time to ask him and chose to respect his request. As for my daughter, she wants us to show our affection toward her regardless of where we are or who's around. We're okay with that!

WRAPPING IT UP . . .

Maybe your tween or teen is like my daughter. You're constantly giving and receiving affection from your child and you love it. That's awesome! Maybe your child is like my son, low key, the "show me the love, but keep it down." That's okay too. Maybe your child doesn't want you to show him physical affection at all.

As difficult as it may be, respect their request. Show your affection in other ways. Text him a nice message like, "Have an awesome day," or "Good luck on your test or game. Proud of you for all the time you spent preparing for it." Send him an inspirational quote or a link to a funny video. Surprise him with his favorite snack.

Maybe you're like me—you've become a little distant and disconnected, assuming that this is what your tween or teens wants you to do. If this is you, please don't make assumptions. Ask your child.

Strategy 2. Provide truthful encouragement.

My son has been playing soccer since he was five-years old. He is very passionate about this sport. He plays outdoor soccer during the fall and spring and indoor soccer during the winter. During soccer season, he usually has two practices on weekdays and a game on the weekends. Now that he's a teenager, I no longer need to stay during practice. I drop him off and pick him up when practice ends. I do, however, attend as many games as I can.

One thing that I've been noticing since my son's first game at the age of five is how players, regardless of how well or badly they play, are cheered by the crowd. Parents and family members are excited about supporting and cheering for their teams whether or not they end up to be the winning team.

I have witnessed a few times a player kicks the ball toward their own team's goal post and parents cheer the player on by crying, "Good job son!" or, "It's okay Alannah!"

Other times, I've witnessed children not being team players, standing in the field, distracting other players, or receiving a yellow or red card—yet their parents tell their children after the game that they did a great job. (Yellow and red cards are used for misconduct during the game.)

I don't know the family dynamics that are taking place in these examples, nor do I intend to judge the way these parents choose to encourage and show support for their children. But I can't stop myself from thinking that the youngsters in these examples are probably aware of their poor performance, because they are either honest with themselves or they were scolded by other team members after the game.

These youngsters were not performing well, yet the adults were cheering them on, giving a false sense of support and encouragement. What are we teaching these youngsters when we tell them it's okay to put in little or no effort?

Truthful Encouragement vs. Cheering Up

As moms, it's engraved in our DNA to provide encouragement to our children. We want them to be happy and successful in everything they do. Whether things are going well or aren't going as planned, we want to be there to cheer them up. Is there such a thing as hurtful encouragement? Is our cheering sending the wrong message to our child? Will this affect my relationship with my tween or teen? After all, encouragement is the action of proving support, confidence, or hope.

When I think about authentic relationships, two things come to my mind—truth and trust. There's no trust if there's no truth. Relationships grow stronger when both parties are truthful to each other and trust one another. When a person is honest with another, they can share truths that will lead to growth and a stronger relationship.

If your best friend is doing something that is preventing her from succeeding, and you know exactly what it is, wouldn't you point it out to her so she can make the necessary changes to make it better? If you are aware of her mistakes, yet you choose to cheer her up instead of pointing out what needs to be addressed, wouldn't you be holding her back?

The same is true with your tween or teen. Each time you cheer on your child when she is not giving her best, are you providing encouragement? Is there a possibility that the message you're sending is that it's okay to be mediocre? Here's a conversation between a mom and her teen that shows this point.

> Mom - Honey, how did you do on the test?
> Teen - It sucked, I totally failed it!
> Mom - Did you prepare for your test?
> Teen - I did during first period.

Mom - Do you think that studying 20 minutes before the
test is enough time to learn all the material?
Teen - I tried my best mom.
Mom - I'm glad you tried your best, honey.

I'm not suggesting that you shouldn't provide encouragement when your child makes a mistake. Frankly, this is
a time when they need encouragement the most. What I'm
suggesting is that rather than cheering them up when they
intentionally mess up, like the example above, provide truthful
encouragement, point out the issue in a non-judgmental way
and allow natural consequences to happen.

Sticking with the example above, mom knows that pro-
crastination and studying for twenty minutes before the test
are not effective study skills. If he keeps doing this, he will
likely fail school. Her son's test results attest to this. Although
her son said that he did his best, you and I know he didn't.
He simply procrastinated and winged the test. Yet, mom
attempted to encourage him by saying "I know you did your
best." Did he?

Perhaps the conversation should have gone something
like this:

Mom - Honey, how did you do on the test?
Teen - It sucked, I totally failed it!
Mom - Did you prepare for your test?
Teen - I did during first period.
Mom - Do you think that studying 20 minutes before the
test is enough time to learn all the material?
Teen - I did my best . . .
Mom - Based on your grade, studying 20 minutes before
the test wasn't enough time to learn the material. Now
you know that studying before the test isn't the best study
strategy. For your next test, I suggest that you make a
study plan. What do you think will work for you?

Teen - I don't know.
Mom - May I give you a suggestion?
Teen - Sure.

After watching my son playing soccer for many years, I can figure out when he is giving his best in the field and when he's tired or slacking. As his mom, I want him to enjoy and succeed in this sport. But I also want him to give his best for the team. Hence, when I know he's not giving his best, I make sure I point it out in a non-judgmental way. "Son, I enjoyed the game today. Although, I noticed you were not into it. You missed a few opportunities and weren't in-tune with the other players. I've seen you play better than this. What's going on?"

Usually, he will answer, "I know, I sucked! I wasn't into it. My head hurt (or whatever reason) . . ." And the conversations will go on.

As you noticed, I started letting him know that I enjoyed the game, not that he did a good job. Next, non-judgmentally, I let him know that he didn't do his best based on the performance I've seen in the past.

WRAPPING IT UP . . .

We moms are our child's #1 fans. As it is, our children are bombarded by negative feedback and messages as they go about their day. It's important that we counteract these messages with love, support, and encouragement so that they can build confidence and succeed. But it has to be honest feedback and truthful encouragement.

You're the mom, and you know them best. When they are being mediocre or winging things—taking the easy way out—it's our responsibility to bring it up and correct this bad habit. If we don't address this issue now, our children will potentially become mediocre adults.

The sad part is, in some instances, they are not even aware of their mediocrity because as children they were never corrected. Avoid telling them "good job" when they didn't do a good job. They know when they don't do a good job.

Starting today, only provide truthful encouragement. Your tween or teen will appreciate your honesty and productive feedback.

Strategy 3. Schedule time to "hang out" with your tween and teen.

What comes to your mind when you hear the phrase, "hang out?" Perhaps you're picturing in your mind a time when you and your best friends were so relaxed, worry-free, having an amazing time.

I'm intentionally using the word "hang out" because that's how I want you to see it—a time you set aside for your tween/teen to enjoy each other's company without an agenda in mind. It's during these special moments that the doors to your youngster's heart and mind open up. Once they let you in, please be tactful. Don't bombard them with questions as if you were a CIA agent in an interrogation room. Instead, relax and have a conversation.

> ONCE A WEEK, FOR AT LEAST THIRTY MINUTES, CLEAR YOUR TIME AND MIND, SHIFT GEARS AND FOCUS ON YOUR SON OR DAUGHTER.

Once a week, for at least thirty minutes, clear your time and mind, shift gears and focus on your son or daughter. If you can, go longer and schedule hang out times more often, please do so. Another option, especially for busy moms who have more children is to schedule shorter hang out times. These hang out times can be as simple as a conversation in the privacy of her room or more complex as to having a candlelight dinner at the local Italian restaurant. The place really doesn't matter.

What really matters is the fact that you're setting time aside to be present, fully engaged, and focused on your youngster.

Find out what works best for you and your youngster. Here are some ideas:

Longer Dates:

1. Dining out

2. Movie night (theatre or your living room)

3. Working out

4. Coffeehouse

5. Walking around downtown or the shopping mall.

6. Game Night with your child or invite their friends over.

7. Picnic at the park or the living room while watching a movie together.

8. Art Night

9. Play outdoor games, hiking, bowling, tennis, paint ball, laser-tag, archery, go-carts, indoor trampoline or rock climbing centers, etc.

10. Massages

11. Visit a museum

12. Attend art galleries and art centers. Most art venues host receptions that are open to the public.

13. Attend a concert.

14. Attend a local live theatre show. Consider the local high school for performances.

15. Take a cooking or art class together

16. Go out for ice cream

17. A walk on the mall.

Shorter Dates:

1. Sit by their bed before bedtime and have a conversation.

2. Ride a bike

3. Go for a Walk/Run

4. Fix hors d'oeuvres together and enjoy them.

5. Cook or bake a recipe together.

6. Do each other's nails and hair.

7. Guided meditation together

8. Complete a project or play video games together.

9. Let your tween/teen decide!

10. Together, listen to your son's top-10 songs. (I know this one might be painful to some moms, but it'll mean a world to your tween or teen.)

If this is a new practice, take the time to introduce the idea to your tween and teen first. Here's a suggestion: "Honey, we've been quite busy lately and I miss spending time with you. I would love to do something together, you and I, every week for about thirty-minutes so, we can stay in touch with each other. I promise it's a pressure-free, zero-interrogation time. What do you say?"

Here are a few tips to make this experience a pleasant one.

1. Be present and mindful.

2. Stay away from communication devices. No calls or texting.

3. Keep in mind this is not an interrogation opportunity.

4. Don't come as a dictator with an agenda in mind. Simply suggest and be willing to listen.

5. If your tween/teen is a limited-talker, start the conversation. Share with him something that happened to you and ask for his feedback. Ask him what he would do if it happened to him?

6. If your tween/teen is upset and doesn't want to hang out today, respect her request. Text her an inspirational quote, a comforting Bible verse, a funny YouTube video, or an amusing meme. When she calms down, pay her a visit in her room.

7. Relax and have fun!

You can also consider spending a few minutes each day to catch up with each other. It doesn't have to be scheduled all the time. Something that I've been doing with my tween and teen since they were in primary school is what I call a daily review.

Basically, a daily review is a five to ten-minute conversation in which we share with each other the highlights of our day. To be honest, the conversations may last between one to thirty minutes based on the mood they're in after school. Since I mainly work from home, I am usually available when my children come home from school. We have our daily review as soon as they arrive. I close my laptop, mute my phone, and listen. I give them my undivided attention.

If you're out when your children come home, you can have your daily review while driving home from their after-school programs and practices, during dinner, or before going to bed. If your children arrive at the same time, give each child time to talk about their day without one interrupting the other. As you give them a few minutes of your day, every day, you're strengthening your relationship and connecting with them authentically.

WRAPPING IT UP . . .

Like any new habit, it will take some time for your youngster to accept that you're being sincere and that you really care about this relationship. Don't make it a habit to cancel or reschedule, as this will only ruin the trust your child has in you. There might be circumstances in which you'll have to reschedule your date. Don't feel guilty about it. Instead, ensure that you follow through. Be persistent and patient. Moms don't quit!

Strategy 4. Simplifying Your Family Life.

> THE WAY WE LIVE OUR LIVES WILL INFLUENCE THE WAY OUR CHILDREN LIVE THEIR LIVES AS ADULTS.

As parents, we set the foundation for our children's lives. We make decisions based on our experience, values, and priorities. From the time our children are young, we begin to pass on our values to them and become their role models. As they grow, our children begin to pay attention to how we live our lives, the decisions we make, how we use our time, how we conduct ourselves, and the things we value the most. Either they adopt, reject, or replace our values and habits (good or bad). The way we live our lives will influence the way our children live their lives as adults.

In the past few years, I've noticed a trend among families. The more I speak with moms, the more they share about their fast-paced lifestyles. I come from a family of ten. When I was a teen, my day involved getting up and ready for school, attending school, playing in the backyard or around the neighborhood, climbing as many trees as I could, doing chores, having dinner, and working on my homework before bedtime.

As a family, we did a few things together such as vacations, game nights, and going to church on Sunday to name a few. We were busy, but it was a slower paced lifestyle. Some of my siblings were involved in extracurricular activities, and others preferred to stay home. My most precious childhood memory is that every evening by 6 o'clock, each of us gathered around the table to have dinner together and share our daily adventures.

I remember having time to chill and for self-discovery, watching movies at the local drive-in, or heading to the beach with my friends to ditch school. Life was good. My dad was a full-time minister at a local church and my mother left her job to become a stay-at-home mother after my oldest brother was born. My point is, most families used to have time to be calm and connect with each other. They set time aside to spend time together, have conversations, eat together, and play games together. They had the same 24 hours each day and 52 weeks per year—just like we do today.

OVERSCHEDULED LIVES

Nowadays, families are living hectic, fast-paced lives. It seems to me, the act of being busy is highly glorified by our culture. Everyone is extremely busy and many seem to wear this badge proudly.

More often than not, when I ask a mom about how her tween or teen is doing, typically her response is: "Jane is keeping herself busy. She's in dance classes three nights a week. She dances for the school's dance team and plays softball for the town's league. She just signed up for the school's drama club and volunteers one afternoon a week at the local animal shelter. She's so busy that I rarely cross paths with her these days."

Today, tweens and teens are busier than ever. From extra-curricular activities, music class, dance class, sports, gaming, spiritual activities, school, volunteering, chores, and work, these youngsters are hopping from one activity to another with no breaks in between.

Some have no choice but to swallow their meals on their way to the next activity whereas others simply skip their meals until they get home and have dinner before heading to bed. Day after day, these youngsters have places to be which consequently leaves limited to no time to calm and relax.

Our youth live overscheduled lives. We then wonder why, according to the U.S. Department of Health and Human Services, approximately one out of five adolescents have a mental health disorder, and nearly one third of them show symptoms of depression[4].

As adults, we are not always well equipped to deal with busyness and the stress that comes along with a fast-paced lifestyle. While keeping a hectic lifestyle can boost brain health, it can also lead to unhealthy levels of stress if we are not careful[5]. Research has shown that high levels of stress can lead to mental health issues such as irritability, anxiety, feeling overwhelmed, and depression.

On the physical health side, stress can increase the risk of coronary heart disease, high cholesterol, high blood pressure, obesity, fatigue, and gastrointestinal complications, to name just a few[6].

If, as adults, we struggle to keep up with hectic lifestyle and maintaining our wellness, how much more difficult can it be for a tween or teen to

> IF, AS ADULTS, WE STRUGGLE TO KEEP UP WITH HECTIC LIFESTYLE AND MAINTAINING OUR WELLNESS, HOW MUCH MORE DIFFICULT CAN IT BE FOR A TWEEN OR TEEN TO MAINTAIN A FAST-PACED LIFESTYLE WITHOUT CONSEQUENTLY FACING A PSYCHOLOGICAL, EMOTIONAL OR PHYSIOLOGICAL BREAKDOWN?

maintain a fast-paced lifestyle without consequently facing a psychological, emotional or physiological breakdown? There's so much our bodies and mind are capable of tolerating without ending up collapsing. And lacking rest or downtime can certainly weaken our mind, body, and soul.

Let me be clear before I move on, I believe that our youth need to be active. We know about the numerous physical and psychological benefits of being active. As they begin to discover their passions, interests, and skills, it's important that we provide them with opportunities to develop and put into practice their abilities and talents. To say the least, our youth thrive on activity.

What I am suggesting is, "too much, too fast, and no free time" is a recipe for overload and burn out. When our youth have limited to no free time in their hands, they're depriving themselves from nurturing their creativity, exploring their potential, developing inner-resources, being innovative, and resting their bodies.

Take a good look at each of your schedules. How do they look? Are you living each day, running from work to driving kids around town to fixing meals? Is your tween or teen booking every day from morning until dusk? Does he have free time or days off? If your answer to the latter question is either *barely* or *not at all*, I would like to recommend you consider simplifying your family's life.

Let me share with you two steps you can take toward simplifying your tween or teen's life: Consistency and Avoid Overbooking. In chapter 8, I'll be sharing with you strategies to help you declutter your life and detoxify your relationships so you can live a simpler and more purposeful life.

Simplifying My Tween/Teen's Life

By now, you're probably thinking: "If you knew my situation, you would know that it's impossible to simplify my son's life." I understand. Some families are busier than others.

My family also lived a hectic lifestyle. My husband Sergio and I worked from nine to five. In addition to school, our daughter was involved in dance, music classes, Girl Scouts, and art classes. Our son was involved in soccer, music classes, school band, and jazz band.

To top it off, my husband and I served on various committees at our church and volunteered for a few local organizations. Between working, taking care of my family's needs, driving kids around town, attending meetings, and volunteering, we were away from home every single night of the week except for Sundays.

Deep inside, I knew that the road we were heading on was unhealthy and dangerous. In the midst of all this, my husband and I made a choice—to simplify our family's life. I learned about the value and benefits of simplifying our lives. I learned that if I don't free up our tween or teen's schedule, I would be depriving them from the opportunity to explore their potential, become in-tune with themselves, experience calm, and enjoy being home.

Now that we are intentional about simplifying our schedules, we are more connected with each other and able to spend more time together while still doing the things we love. As a result, our son has recently discovered his new passion for photography and our daughter has time to make squishies and promote her online store.

Why are tween or teen's schedules overbooked? As I speak about this issue with parents, some have shared with me that they want to expose their child to as many experiences as possible during their childhood and adolescent years. Others want their tweens to explore opportunities so that they can discover their passions and potential. Often times, parents have shared the fact that they're thinking ahead about possible financial opportunities available for college that their teen can benefit from.

These are legitimate reasons. But keep in mind that the busier your youngster is, the less time he has available to be in-tune with his inner-self and be able to connect authentically with his family.

Let's start by clarifying that this is not a quick fix. Rather, it's a lifestyle change that starts with committing to taking small steps toward a less cluttered life. The busier your youngster's schedule is, the more time she may require to simplify it. As they simplify their lives, these youngsters will have fewer distractions, less pressure, more focus, and the opportunity to be better in-tune with their well-being.

Step 1. Consistency

As I work with parents, they often share their frustration with consistency. After all, life is unpredictable and there's no such thing as a typical day. We make plans, but we can't always control the circumstances that surround us. We can, however, provide consistency in the areas that are under our control. There's one thing most tweens and teens agree on—they need consistency.

In the book, *Simplicity Parenting*, author Kim John Payne suggests that increasing the rhythm of your home life is one of the most powerful ways of simplifying your children's lives. He adds that relationships are built when nothing much is going on[7].

Children and youth need consistency in their lives. Why is consistency so important for our youngsters? Consistency creates security, expectancy, dependability, and peace of mind. They want to know what to expect and the consequences of these expectations.

Here are four tips to provide consistency in your youngster's life even during those busy days.

Tip 1. Preview next week's schedule.

At the beginning of each week, go over the family schedule with your children. I usually do this on Sunday evening during dinner or before we go to bed. A word of advice—avoid coming across as a dictator. Simply share the schedule and allow them to give their input. Sometimes, adjustments can be made in the schedule to meet everyone's needs. Yet there are times when activities in the schedule are non-negotiable. And that's okay.

I don't know about your tween or teen, but my son and daughter suffer from selective amnesia. They tend to remember everything related to their wants and needs. Yet things that don't fit in their agenda have no place in their memory.

To avoid any misunderstandings, I also give them daily updates and reminders. Depending on their schedules, I either remind them during the evening following our devotion time or before they leave the house in the morning. My children appreciate these weekly and daily reminders because it helps them plan accordingly. They also know what to expect on that particular week, creating stability and peace of mind.

Tip 2. Synchronize your family schedules.

There are a few ways to synchronize your schedules. Each family member can have a printed version of the weekly calendar they can post on the refrigerator or on a board in their room. You can also print a small-size copy of the week's schedule they can tape on their school's agenda.

Another idea is synchronizing your phone calendars. There are apps that allow you to synchronize the calendars of those in the family plan. Create a family calendar everyone is able to access. Usually these apps update instantly. This will help each family member have instant access to the schedule and be able to update it right on the spot.

Tip 3. Do certain activities consistently.

In our home, we eat dinner together as often as we possibly can. We have been pretty consistent about this practice since our children were born. However, there are a few nights in which not everyone can be home at dinnertime. Regardless, those who are home sit at the table. Another activity we do together is devotions before heading to bed. At 9:15 p.m., everyone gathers in our bedroom for devotions and prayer.

Some families find it easier to have breakfast together and others have certain rituals before they leave the house or before they go to bed. One mom told me that her family has quiet time before bedtime. The kids work on their homework while the parents read for pleasure.

Tip 4. Provide consistent discipline.

When I was practicing as a psychologist, more often than not, youngsters would share their frustration about inconsistent discipline at home. They would say that mom allowed them to stay until 10 p.m. at their friend's home. Yet dad would get upset because he expected them to be home by 9 p.m. Other youngsters told how dad cared less about how much time they spent playing videos games, but mom would scold them for playing video games for hours.

Then, there are a few teens that appreciated the inconsistent discipline because they were able to get away with things without a consequence. Needless to say, tweens and teens agreed that inconsistent discipline drove them crazy because boundaries were not clear and they didn't know what to expect.

Frankly, no one can be consistent all the time. And, it's pretty hard to stay consistent. However, there's a danger with being frequently inconsistent. Your child's behavior may escalate, and you'll likely be seen as less of an authority. When we are inconsistent in our discipline, we're sending mixed messages and confusing our child. Consequently, we're hurting our relationship with them.

If this is an area that needs improvement in your family, I have two suggestions for you. First, take the time to discuss this issue with your partner. Respectfully, identify the areas in which both of you are not providing consistency in discipline. As a team, talk about the reasons behind the inconsistency and come up with a mutual agreement. Secondly, tackle one behavior issue you're experiencing with your child at a time. Work on that specific behavior and when, corrected, move on to the next one. Keep in mind that addressing too many behaviors at once can create confusion and overwhelm.

I know that there are family dynamics in which consistent discipline from both parents is simply impossible. You may not be able to control the way your child's father disciplines her, especially when he lives in a different home. You can, however, control the way you discipline her when she's with you.

> CONSISTENT DISCIPLINE
> CREATES BOUNDARIES,
> LIMITS, EXPECTATIONS
> AND ACCOUNTABILITY.

It's important that you mean what you say. Otherwise, what you say starts to lose its meaning. I understand that there will be circumstances in which you might have to adjust your discipline style. As much as you can, I encourage you to stick to your decisions and be consistent. Consistent discipline creates boundaries, limits, expectations and accountability.

I encourage you to find what works for your family. As much as you possibly can, practice consistent discipline. Boundaries, rules, expectations, and consequences must be clear and consistent. Talk to your child and ask for her input. Start by letting her know the reasons why you would like to simplify her life. Let her know that as she declutters her schedule, she'll be able to take a break from busyness, be more in-tune with her inner-self, experience consistency, less stress, and peace of mind. You'll be surprised as to how much she longs for simplicity and consistency.

Step 2. Teach your Tween/Teen The Art of Not Overbooking

When my husband Sergio and I realized how crowded the lives of our children were, the first thing we did was sit down with them and talk about the consequences should we stay that busy and the benefits of simplifying their lives. We asked them to list on a piece of paper every activity they're involved in and rank them based on preference.

Next, we asked them to pick one activity that they were willing to let go of so they could live a less hectic lifestyle. In case they would refuse to select one activity, our plan B was to let go of the last activity on their list. To our surprise, each selected one or two activities they were willing to let go of without complaining.

Do you want to know why they were willing to give up some activities willingly? They were actually feeling overwhelmed. My husband and I joined them by doing the same exercise and also let go of a few commitments.

Some commitments required a simple email to cancel, whereas others needed a more transitional approach. Regardless, taking this step opened up a few nights for us, which we really appreciated.

Here are two tips to help your tween or teen avoid overbooking themselves:

Tip 1. Minimize Commitments.

As they grow, new activities and opportunities will present themselves. If your daughter wants to be in the dance team next school year, ask her, "Which present commitment(s) are you willing to give up to accommodate this new activity in your schedule?" This will teach her to be selective, replace one activity with another, and avoid overbooking that often leads to stress.

Tip 2. Set Time Aside for Downtime

Rest is essential to avoid physical and psychological exhaustion. As demands increase in their lives and there's not enough rest, our children are putting at risk their physical and emotional wellness. Consequently, they're functioning under auto-pilot.

Have you been in a high school classroom during the first or second period? It's like watching a zombie vs. alien movie. These kids are so zoned out in the mornings that aliens can be taking over the high school and they wouldn't even notice it until they found themselves caged inside a spacecraft for human research.

What concerns me the most is, due to exhaustion, they're missing instruction and not performing at their best. Not only is rest essential to function in life, it also increases attention, focus, innovation, and learning.

Let me share with you three ideas to encourage your tween or teen to schedule downtime.

Idea 1. Block downtime on your schedule.
If your daughter or son has a hectic schedule, I strongly recommend scheduling evenings off. Whether it's one, two, or three evenings a week, a break in-between a hectic schedule is simply good practice, which is essential for their wellness.

We want to teach our children the art of not overbooking themselves to prevent physical and emotional distress that comes along with ongoing busyness. Block out at least one day per week for no extracurricular activities.

Some families block Sundays as their day of rest. Other families, like ours, select one or two nights each week for no extracurricular activities. Having nights off between weekdays breaks the busyness cycle and teaches your youngster that it's okay to not be busy all the time. It also frees the schedule for spontaneous adventures like going to the ice cream shop for a scrumptious banana split or caramel sundae.

Initially, they may complain about boredom. No worries, don't let their complaining get to you. They will eventually figure out what to do during the nights off. They'll find themselves not needing to rush through their homework. They'll even have some extra time to chill and listen to music. Keep in mind that you're not their event planner. Let them figure out how to enjoy their evenings off.

Idea 2. Schedule a "lights-out" time.
Bedtimes vary from teen to teen based on different factors. However, it's important that they learn to be disciplined and stop all activities at the end of the day to rest. Begin by helping them understand that it's unhealthy to deprive themselves from resting. In our home, lights are out at 10 p.m. and everyone head to their bedrooms. They might not fall asleep right away. Nonetheless, they're developing self-control and giving themselves the opportunity to wind down at the end of the day.

Idea 3. Limit screen time and phone access.
Today's teens are spending an endless number of hours on their phone. According to a poll by Common Sense Media, a nonprofit focused on educating children, parents, teachers, and policymakers about media and technology, one out of two teens feel addicted to their mobile devices (phone and internet usage) and nearly 80% of teens check their phones hourly[8].

Maybe this tip can be a tough one to swallow for your tween or teen. This is when your son or daughter tells you that you're wasting your time reading this book and they will go as far as to tell you that you should find yourself a hobby or something else to do. They might hide the book or post it in Amazon for resale. They're not going to be happy about it, but believe me; it's crucial that we set boundaries over their screen usage. I encourage you to set some rules on phone usage if you haven't done so yet. Here are some suggestions to help you implement this change:

1. Schedule activities in which the cell phone can't be used such as a "device-free dinner." This includes mom and

dad as well. We have to model the behavior we want to see in our children. And if you don't, your tween will scold you for the rest of your days.

2. Schedule time for the phone to be off. In our home, devices must be turned off at 9:30 p.m. during the school year. During the summer, devices are off from 10:30 p.m. to 10:00 a.m. the next day.

3. Search software programs that block the phone from being used.

4. Have a phone station where phones are dropped off at the time you select. If they use their phone alarm to get up in the morning, no worries. They can purchase an alarm clock at the local store.

Wrapping it Up . . .

There's no doubt—youth thrive on activity. A healthy level of activity is essential to boost their physical, emotional, and psychological wellness. As moms, we can help our daughters and sons avoid the toxic trend of overbooking themselves. Simplifying, consistency, and frequent downtime are healthier options to help them release tension while also serving as a break from the pressures of daily life. As our youngsters learn to avoid overbooking, it will open free time they can use to relax, explore, create, innovate, self-reflect, and strengthen relationships with those they care about.

"There's no way to be a perfect mother, but a million ways to be a great one."

—JILL CHURCHILL

2

FOSTERING OPEN COMMUNICATION AND INTENTIONAL LISTENING

"If parenthood came with a GPS it would mostly just say 'recalculating'!"

—SIMON HOLLAND

As our children enter the pre- and adolescent years, suddenly, the opinion of a bunch of tweens or teens is considered as 'the greatest source of wisdom.' They go from being an open book to talking less and less with you and become more involved with peers. Although less communication with parents can be a sign of independency, if we're not careful, our influence is at risk.

Youth have become the target for conflicting messages

MORE THAN EVER, FOSTERING OPEN COMMUNICATION AND INTENTIONAL LISTENING BETWEEN YOU AND YOUR CHILD ARE ESSENTIAL TO MAINTAINING A HEALTHY CONNECTION WITH THEM.

and unhealthy choices. These youngsters are bombarded with conflicting messages intended to confuse them so others could take advantage of their vulnerability. More than ever, fostering open communication and intentional listening between you and your child are essential to maintaining a healthy connection with them. Whether communication between you and your tween or teen is pretty good or needs a little boost, there is always room for improvement. In this chapter, I'm sharing a few ways to foster open communication between you and your child, and adopt intentional listening.

Before we continue, I would like to invite you to ease your body and mind, and relax for a moment. One thing you will hear from me over and over is, as moms, we must take care of ourselves so we can be better able to help our family.

Here's a quick and simple breathing exercise to help you regroup before you continue reading. Begin this exercise by finding a comfortable position. You're welcome to sit on a chair, sit on the floor bringing your feet together into a butterfly position, or lay on your back comfortably.

Breathe in . . . one, two, three . . . hold . . . one, two . . . breathe out . . . one, two, three.

Again, let's breathe in . . . one, two, three, hold . . . one, two, three . . . breath out . . . one, two, three.

Continue to breathe slowly and release areas of tension, feel your muscles relax. Let your worries drift away. Let your breathing relax you.

Breathe in again . . . one, two, three . . . hold . . . one, two . . . breath out . . . one, two, three . . .

Breathe in . . . one, two, three . . . hold . . . one, two . . . breath out . . . one, two, three . . .

Repeat as needed.

Now that you're feeling better and more focused, let's move on.

FOSTERING OPEN COMMUNICATION

You and I know about the importance of having open communication with our tween or teen. Today, our children have unlimited access to so much information through the web whether it's good, bad, or ugly. They have access to the web anytime, anywhere from most electronic devices. Information is at the touch of a button or a click away. As much as we try to restrict or supervise our children, we can't always control what they're exposed to every moment of the day.

We can, however, teach our children to be smart about it and make the right choices. We can also be our youngster's #1 influencer by nurturing trust and healthy boundaries.

Sometimes, we can be a little pushy and overcritical with our children. Without even noticing it, we are distancing ourselves from them. Other times, we simply don't know what to do to connect with them. If you're finding yourself struggling with open communication between you and your tween or teen, I would love to share with you four strategies I use to foster open communication between my tween and teen. The exciting part is that I've actually learned the strategies from children by simply asking them.

1. Be Present.

By now, you've learned about the value of simplifying your tween or teen's life by decluttering their schedule. Now, it's time to focus on being present as a way of connecting with them in a meaningful way. Being present doesn't mean that you're in a stand-by position waiting for your child to make a request or dropping everything you're doing each time your tween or teen wants something from you. Being present means to be intentional about staying involved in your child's life and being mindful while you're spending time with her. In other words, during those ten or fifteen minutes you're spending with your child, you're all hers.

If your tween or teen is like mine, they usually want to talk with you when you're the busiest. I was in the middle of writing chapter 1 of this book quite inspired as I was typing my thoughts into my computer. Suddenly, she stood right in front of me staring and eagerly waiting for me to stop what I was doing to pay attention to what she had to say.

See, my daughter is into making squishy toys. If you're not familiar with squishies, you're a lucky mom! These are toys shaped in various characters or shapes made of soft material, such as memory foam. Kids collect them so they can smoosh and squeeze them over and over again.

My daughter will tell you squishies are stress reliever toys to help children manage their tension—quite convincing! She's so into these toys that she has her own online store at Etsy and her YouTube channel in which she reviews squishies and also teaches kids to make their own.

As I am typing, mind you I'm super into my train of thoughts, she stands in front of me quite fidgety with, not one or two but, five brand new squishies in her hands. She not only wants to show me the brand new squishies she just finished making, but also wants me to squeeze each of them and rate them as either normal or slow rising.

At that moment, I was in the middle of a thought and needed total concentration. I told my daughter, "I really want to check out your squishes and would be happy to squeeze them, but right now I'm in the middle of a thought. I need to finish this so I can give you my undivided attention and take the time to really feel each squishy. Can we do this after I'm done?"

Although she agreed with my request, I could tell she was quite disappointed. I finished the paragraph I was working on and, as we agreed, I asked her to show me the squishes. I'm sure you're dying to know how I rated her hand-made squishies. They all were under the slow raising category.

The truth is, we need to be present for our children. Just like my squishies story above, I'm not suggesting that you have to stop everything you're doing each time your child comes to you wanting your attention. After all, you want them to learn critical life lessons like, "The world doesn't revolve around you, there's time for everything and, sometimes, you just have to wait." But, please make sure that if this is the case, you follow through on the conversation you promised your child. Don't let them wait on you and end up not having the conversation.

Although we want our tween and teen to learn the art of waiting, it's equally important that you evaluate the situation. There are situations in which we have to be flexible. We have to distinguish between things that can wait and conversations that require prompt attention.

Ask yourself; "Is this something urgent that needs immediate attention?" Perhaps your son has been a little distant lately, yet he comes to you for advice while you're doing your nails. If this is the case, perhaps, putting things aside and listening to your tween or teen may be the right thing to do. If this is something that can wait like my daughter's squishies testing session while I was in the middle of my aha moment, teach your tween or teen there are times when they have to wait.

The bottom line is this, we have to be fully present when we are having a conversation with our tween or teen. This means during the conversation, there's no answering phone calls (unless an emergency merits your attention), no browsing social media, no checking emails, or no watching television. They know when you're not present and, they resent it.

You want your child to be able to turn to you when they have problems or when they need to talk. That's why I encourage you to be present, listen and show your child that what he has to say truly matters to you.

2. Use Your "Indoor" Voice.

We're always telling children to use their indoor voice. Whether it's at school, church, movie theatre, or the local grocery store, we want them to learn self-control. When I was working for a school system, one of my offices was located by the school's main entrance. I can't tell you how many times a day, I had to remind students to use their indoor voice while they were inside the school.

These kids had a hard time speaking softly while they were walking down the hallway. Boy, I wish I had a voice recorder that I could play over and over again, "Please use your indoor voice." At the end of the day, we want kids to understand that yelling is unnecessary and learn how to control their tone of voice.

What about us, moms? Do we need to borrow a voice recorder to remind ourselves to use our indoor voice? Sometimes conversations can get a little heated. I know! You just looked online at your son's gradebook I found out that he's got an "F" on his report card. You ask him how come there's an "F" on his report card and he blames it mostly on how his teacher doesn't know how to teach. You're not only disappointed, but also upset that your son is not taking responsibility for his actions. Naturally, you get angry and perhaps your tone of voice begins to escalate. He's upset at you because you're yelling at him and begins to raise his voice.

To say the least, the conversation becomes a war zone with no winners to crown. I've been there and done that. Early in my motherhood, I learned that raising my voice to the point of yelling neither resolves issues nor modifies behavior.

When my oldest son was 5 and youngest daughter was 3, my husband and I decided that we, as parents, needed a parent evaluation. After all, most people receive performance evaluations at work with the goal of identifying personal strengths and pinpoint areas that need improvement.

My husband and I sat on our family room's black couch during a cold winter stormy Saturday morning. We started a fire on our fireplace and called our children downstairs to join us for a meeting. Our son knew how meetings ran since, in the past, he had attended quite a few meetings with us.

On the other hand, our 3-years old daughter was too young to understand what on earth was going on. She simply sat down next to me, looking at me with her big round brown eyes waiting to hear what I had to "Kids," I said, "Papa and I need to know if we are doing a good job as your mom and dad. We want to know how we can be better parents to you." As the brave mom I am, I asked first, "What is your favorite thing about me?"

We let them answer the question and listened to what they had to say. Our son said that he likes when I cook for him. Poor child, he doesn't know better. I'm not that great of a cook. Our daughter was next. She said in her sweet gentle voice: "I like it when you cuddle with me." Then, they went on to say the things they like about their dad.

Next, I asked the question, "What is the thing you don't like that much about me?" Our son was very quick to answer: "When you yell at us. It really scares me and my sister."

Speaking of a weapon of mass destruction! I felt like a bomb just hit me. How can my own children be scared of me? I am their protector; #1 fan and I only want what's best for them. I am their mom. Yet, I was unintentionally hurting my children. That day, I decided to stop yelling at my children.

If you've been catching yourself yelling at your tween and teen too often, know that you're not the only one. It happens and there's no need to punish yourself. Starting today, be more intentional about this issue. Let me share with you three tips to help you as you work toward improving in this area:

1. Like any unhealthy habit, it takes time to replace it with a healthier one. Start by intentionally working on yelling less and less. Be in-tune with yourself and be conscious about not losing control when you're upset. During a heated conversation, repeat to yourself, "I'm in control. I'm staying calm."

2. Partner up with someone (significant other or a close friend) to help you identify when your voice is escalating. In my attempt to eliminate my yelling, I asked my husband to gently touch my arm or hand as a sign that I am escalating and need to cool off. When you find yourself yelling, regain control, stop yourself, take a deep breath and continue talking using an "indoor" voice.

3. It's okay to apologize for yelling unnecessarily. Your tween or teen will admire your honesty and courage to admit a wrongdoing.

Now, I am intentional about using my indoor voice, especially during heated conversations. When we use our indoor voice, and keep it that way, the likelihood that a conversation becomes a war zone is pretty slim. You're not only modeling proper communication skills, but also self-control.

Yes, staying in control can be challenging at times. But I can tell you that, the more intentional you are about it, the easier it gets. No matter how angry I get, I have to be conscious about keeping my voice down. Believe me, I don't always have it right. Just like you, it's a work in progress. Always use your indoor voice, stay in control, and when your daughter raises her voice, calmly ask her to lower it. "I'm keeping my voice down and I'd appreciate if you do the same."

3. Build, Nurture, and Model Trust.
Trust is a two-way street. It defines a relationship. We want our children to trust us just like our children want us to trust them. Yet, trust isn't something that magically appears. It's earned. We earn our children's trust just like they have to earn our trust. When we take the time to build, nurture, and model trust, we're strengthening the bond between mom and child.

As a mom, it's an amazing feeling to see your tween or teen coming to you for advice or to share her deepest thoughts.

It's during these moments that you have the opportunity to influence, advise, or simply listen to your child. All this is possible when there's trust.

As I said before, trust is a two-way street. Sometimes, we assume that our youngsters understand the meaning of trust. It's our responsibility to not only teach but also model trust. Research has shown that tweens and teens need parents to uphold clear boundaries, maintain family rules and values, while encouraging competence and maturity[9]. Once they know the boundaries and expectations, there shouldn't be room for excuses or misunderstandings.

I can't promise that they won't try to pull a stunt or convince you that they didn't know they weren't supposed to take the car without your permission. But, when rules and expectations are clear and consistently enforced, you can come back and say, "I've been pretty clear about our family's rules. You know you can't take the car without my permission. I want to trust you. But, each time you choose to not follow the rules, our relationship takes a toll."

A mom once shared with me, in her effort to build trust between her and her teen daughter, she decided to treat the relationship as if they were best friends. She began to talk and dress like her daughter. She thought, "If I become her best friend, she'll trust me and share her life with me." Unfortunately, this is not a healthy approach.

Tweens and teens want and need a parent. And, often times, this approach doesn't lead to trust. There's a difference between being there for your child as a parent and being your child's friend. When your tween or teen sees you as a friend, boundaries are crossed.

He will not see the need to respect you and follow your

> BEING AND ACTING LIKE A CARING AND RESPONSIBLE PARENT WILL LIKELY INCREASE YOUR DAUGHTER OR SON'S RESPECT, TRUST AND ADMIRATION TOWARD YOU.

directions because, in his head, you're no longer under the "grown up category." You're his friend, and, frankly, you fool around with friends. Being and acting like a caring and responsible parent will likely increase your daughter or son's respect, trust and admiration toward you.

A parent earns trust each time she keeps her word, follows through on her commitments, treats others with respect and compassion, and stands firm on her values and beliefs. She also earns trust when she's truthful, slow to judge, and disciplines with fairness and compassion. It's not about focusing on becoming your child's best friend. It's about being a dependable, trustworthy, and caring parent.

As you work toward building and nurturing trust between you and your child, be careful about trusting your tween or teen so much that you no longer provide the guidance and boundaries they still need. Also, watch for the tendency to under-trust your child, becoming overly intrusive, and suspicious about every move they make. Keep in mind these tendencies can hurt the relationship and counteract your attempt to foster an open communication between you and your child.

My husband and I have taught our children the rules, boundaries, and expectations of our family. When necessary, we take a moment to refresh their memories. My approach has been, "I trust you unless proven otherwise."

When my son asked me if he could date this girl, I sat down with him and went over the rules and expectations of dating (we also revisited 'the talk'). I said, "I'm expecting that you will respect these rules. If you agree and commit to following the rules, I don't have a problem with you dating. On the other hand, if rules are broken, consequences will follow." Clear and straight to the point!

Life isn't always rainbows and unicorns, especially during this challenging developmental stage. There will be times in which trust will be broken, intentionally or accidentally.

When trust is broken between you and your child, don't feel despair. If your tween or teen made a poor choice that led to lack of trust, tell him what he can do to regain your trust. Be specific, firm, and conscious about possible circumstances that could prevent him from regaining trust such as distractions or over-commitments. Instead of scolding him for breaking the trust, have a conversation with him. Address the issue and ensure him you want to trust him but he has to put forth effort to regain your trust.

It's important that we discipline our children and allow natural consequences that result from their poor choices. When they make a mistake, avoid telling them, "I'll never trust you again," as this can only hurt the relationship and potentially eliminate any desire to make amends. Also, help you child make amends, apologize, and re-build trust in the relationship. Forgiveness is as important as discipline.

4. Don't Lecture Your Tween/Teen. Instead, Have a Conversation.

I often hear parents say: "My teen doesn't want to talk with me." But frankly, it's more like "My teen doesn't want to listen to me." It takes two to tango. Likely, it takes at least two to have a conversation (Although, some of us don't mind self-talk).

There's a difference between having a conversation and lecturing someone. Do you remember when you were a teen and your parents kept lecturing you about how bad your boyfriend was and how he will ruin your life? They kept going on and on about your wild boyfriend. They would bring him up (and remind you about how much they hated him!) every time they could—even when the conversation was originally about how annoying uncle Bill was during last night's dinner. I bet you totally tuned them out and likely told yourself, "I don't care what they think!" Don't let this happen to your tween or teen.

If you're in the habit of making a lecture out of every conversation, don't be surprised when your tween or teen tunes you out. I encourage you to resist the temptation to talk at them. Instead, talk with them and be mindful during the conversation. Make sure it's a two-way conversation. Ask questions and, as I said before, listen.

Let me be clear before we go on. There are situations in which we have to correct our daughter or son right on the spot. Say, your family is having dinner and your 5-year-old daughter accidentally spills your teen son's glass of water on the table.

Immediately, your son yells at her, "I hate you! I can't wait until the day you disappear from earth and I don't have to ever see you again." Of course, you can't ignore this behavior. And based on his harsh words, correcting him along with a reminder about your family's values and beliefs is in place.

We should not be inclined to lecture our kids each time they come to us with an issue or a problem. Just because your 12-years old daughter shares with you that she is concerned about her best friend because she's been watching pornography online and sexting with some boys from school, doesn't mean that this is the right time to lecture your daughter about the dangers of sexting and pornography while pulling out extensive data that proves why she should stay away from these evils.

Perhaps, what your daughter needs at this moment is some advice to help her friend overcome this issue. "Honey, it means a lot to me that you're sharing your best friend's problem with me. Let's talk about how you can help her stop watching pornography and sexting."

WRAPPING IT UP . . .

The truth is, there will always be ups and downs in a relationship. Sometimes, small disappointments can result in healthier bonds. I encourage you and your child to be willing to try again and again and not give up as you both work on regaining each other's trust. And, above all, adopt intentional listening and be slow to make judgments and assumptions.

ADOPTING INTENTIONAL LISTENING

Many tweens and teens complain their parents don't give them a chance to speak. They claim that parents often jump to conclusions quickly and lose their temper instantly. You know, they're mostly right. Frankly, some moms are more patient and tolerant than others. Once, I was with my son at the doctor's office, waiting to be seen. As we found our seats on the waiting room, a mom walked in with her teen daughter. After they checked in, they sat one chair down from us. Since they were sitting so close to us, I was able to hear their conversation.

The daughter, with teary eyes, was telling her mom that while she was taking a test on the computer, her friend texted her answers to some of the questions. The daughter was honest and told her mother that she copied a few answers and how bad she felt for doing it. The mom hugged her, thanked her for her honesty and told her that, once they got home, they would think about how to handle the situation and make things right.

Not all moms react like the one in the doctor's office. Some tend to be more impulsive and judgmental than others. And, when we ask for an explanation, by the time our son opens his mouth to make his statement, we have already bombarded him with accusations, assumptions, and a list of past offenses. I know, I've been there, done that—sigh. Tweens and teens really dislike when we make assumptions about them that are not true.

Do conversations between you and your tween or teen go somewhat like this?

Mom - "Why didn't you wash your dishes after dinner today?"
Daughter - <Sigh>
Mom - "I know what you're doing. I wasn't born yesterday missy. For the past 13 years, I've been telling you, *every*

45

day, that you have to wash your dishes. But no, you *never* listen. You're *always* in la la land or on your phone. I'm tired of telling you this *every* day. After all these years, you keep doing the same thing. Will you ever learn your lesson?"

Daughter - <Staring at mom upset and breathing deeply.>

Needless to say, research has shown that listening to your tween or teen's thoughts, feelings, concerns, ideas, perspectives, experiences, and interests significantly improves the relationship between parent and child[10].

If being intentional about listening is crucial for a healthy and strong relationship with our tween or teen, why is it so challenging? According to the Merriam-Webster Dictionary, being intentional means to be determined to act in a certain way.[11]. Intentional listening is as simple as to focus on the conversation, be present and listen carefully to what your child has to say without interrupting her. If your tween or teen is somewhat like mine, sometimes you need clarification.

If you have a question or need clarification, don't keep it to yourself. If you refrain from asking or clarifying, what may happen is that you could end up making assumptions about a conclusion you've made without clarifying first. Wait until they're done or politely interrupt to get clarification.

Tweens and teens want to be taken seriously, especially by their parents. Listen to their point of view, even if it's difficult to hear what they have to say. It's when they can count on you to share their mistakes without being afraid of being scolded or judged that the relationship steps up to the next level. Let them complete their thoughts before you respond.

One thing I find quite helpful is repeating what you hear them say to ensure you understand it correctly. "Let me make sure I'm understanding what you're saying. I hear you saying . . . Is this right?"

Here are six tips you're welcome to consider as you adopt intentional listening into your parenting style:

1. Let your tween or teen tell the whole story before intervening or taking sides.

2. When you ask a question, be quiet and listen. Don't interrupt or talk over your child. Let him speak. When we listen, we're modeling basic communication skills and showing respect to our child. Whether you believe him or not, don't interrupt or scold him. Instead, speak with him.

3. Avoid using words like *never, always,* and *every.* Chances are the statement isn't accurate. Can you always be happy? Can you never be upset? These words tend to imply extremes, twist things around, and can potentially create tension and distrust between you and your child.

4. Don't try to immediately excuse, magnify, minimize, or fix the situation.

5. Brainstorm solutions or possibilities. Keep in mind that because you're listening doesn't mean you're agreeing with her.

6. If your assumptions were wrong, apologize to your tween or teen. This shows character while modeling good manners. I've found that when I apologize to my child, her respect and admiration toward me gets stronger!

As I briefly mentioned above, making assumptions and being judgmental can potentially hurt or destroy the relationship between you and your child. When you show a confrontational or judgmental attitude about the poor decisions or misbehaviors your tween or teen display, they will immediately turn you off. Tweens and teens are very sensitive to this kind of attitude. As much as you may try, you can't hide your judgment, no matter how seemingly subtle it may be.

Here are five tips to stay in-tune with yourself and avoid judgmental thoughts:

1. Pay attention to your body language and tone of voice.

2. Encourage your child to speak openly. For this to happen, you want to be open-minded, hold on to your opinions until she has finished, and avoid judgmental statements ("You can't even control yourself—can you?") or blaming ("You're always making poor choices.").

3. Be empathetic. Put yourself in your child's shoes. Remember, it was just yesterday when you were also an adolescent. Even when you don't necessarily agree, communicate that you're listening and you understand what she's going through.

4. Correct the behavior, address the issue and make suggestions as needed in a loving and compassionate way.

5. Remind your child that you love her and appreciate her honesty and trust despite of the particular incident or choice made.

WRAPPING IT UP . . .

Open communication and intentional listening don't always come naturally. It takes work! Mom, keep in mind that if you're adopting a new way of doing things, it will take some time to kick in. At the beginning, it might feel a little awkward or uncomfortable. Don't push it. Instead, be patient with yourself, persistent and sensitive to their reaction. Remember, moms don't quit!

> *"My kids call it "yelling" when I raise my voice. I call it Motivational speaking of the selective listener."*

—UNKNOWN AUTHOR

3

HEALTHY DISCIPLINING: BEYOND TAKING AWAY AND PUNISHMENT

"Don't let yourself become so concerned with raising a good kid that you forget you already have one."

—GLENNON MELTON

As moms, we know the value of disciplining our children. At the end of the day, we want to raise a youngster with character, self-control, self-discipline, and respect. For years, parents have relied on taking away things, punishment, and grounding as forms of discipline. Others use spanking in their attempt to stop undesired behaviors.

Although, I've met a small number of parents who swear by these techniques, many moms have expressed their frustration with taking away and grounding, especially when it comes to disciplining their tween or teen. Even if this type of discipline worked during the younger years, parents who rely on punishment to control their kids realize that something needs to change now that they're older.

When our son was a preschooler, I used time-outs and spanking very sporadically. Since, it was so rare, he reacted when I did it. Granted, the few occasions he was spanked were due to the same reason—he blatantly disrespected me in public. Even though he was punished for his naughty behavior, he repeated the same behavior at a later time.

Why does this kid repeat the same behavior after being punished? Does he like punishment? I pondered. That's when I realized that punishment alone wasn't the answer. I did not need to tell him to stop the naughty behavior. Instead, I needed to teach the behavior I wanted to see in him and help him understand why this behavior is better than the undesired behavior. Since then, I've been avoiding punitive discipline with both of my children. I haven't used spanking anymore (our daughter got lucky!), and we don't ground our children. We do, however, set boundaries, give them clear expectations, teach and model desired behavior and foster a safe-zone where they can freely share their successes and mistakes without fear. Yes, we also believe in consequences.

> INSTEAD, I NEEDED TO TEACH THE BEHAVIOR I WANTED TO SEE IN HIM AND HELP HIM UNDERSTAND WHY THIS BEHAVIOR IS BETTER THAN THE UNDESIRED BEHAVIOR.

I'm not here to rate or judge the way you discipline your child. My goal is to share with you discipline options that have worked for me and other parents I've worked with. Maybe you want to tweak or adjust the way you discipline your child after you finish reading this chapter. Small changes can reap tremendous results. See, when you take away things or ground your child to a doomed sentence away from the rest of the world, more often than not, this fails to change or correct the undesired behavior. Frankly, it creates anger and resentment toward you.

If you are facing this challenge right now with your

daughter or son, there's no need to feel defeated. Take your time as you read this chapter and go over the exercises found in the workbook that accompanies this book. Give yourself time to reflect on your answers and decide what's best for your family.

Setting Clear Boundaries and Expectations

Most tweens and teens have an internal desire to impress their parents and earn their approval. They love when you encourage and motivate them, even if they don't show it or tell you. They also thrive for boundaries and clear expectations. The clearer we are with our child, the less room for tension and confusion.

Let's think about this for a moment. Say, you're starting a new job. It's your first day at the job and your supervisor welcomes you warmly. She gives you a tour of the building and finally walks you to your new office. As she walks away, she tells you, "Good luck! You're on your own."

Although you're quite impressed with your new office, your anxiety level is raising quickly. You're clueless about the expectations, boundaries, what's acceptable or what's not. Suddenly, your excitement turns into massive stress and anxiety. Now, you're walking on eggshells hoping you don't mess up and get fired for doing something you didn't know you shouldn't.

Our children go through the same feelings, thoughts and inner-struggles when we aren't clear about our expectations and boundaries.

"My mom has never told me I can't watch R-rated movies."

"I don't even know what my mom thinks about me watching porn."

"I stay up late playing videogames every night. My mom doesn't say anything."

"I go to bed whenever I want. My mom hasn't told me I have a bedtime."

Before we expect any form of discipline to work, we have to set a solid foundation by communicating clear expectations and setting healthy boundaries. Once you communicate expectations and boundaries, share with your tween or teen the reasons why you're setting them. If you come down like a sledge hammer or claim your throne, you can count on rebellion.

Your child will question your choices and possibly become defiant. There should be a reason or purpose behind your decisions. Whether it's to instill good habits, avoid a failure, develop character, or teach responsibility, it's important that you're clear and pass on your intentions to your child. At the end of the day, you want your daughter or son to follow your lead not fear, defy or resent you.

Even when you share your reasons with your daughter or son, don't be surprised if they question your motives. Until they believe it's the right thing for them to do, they'll likely think you've been unfair. Before you get to that point, it's important that you set boundaries and define expectations first.

What behaviors are acceptable and unacceptable? What expectations do you have for your daughter or son? What is allowed and not allowed? What circumstances are open for negotiation and what's not? Make sure you take the time to let your tween or teen know your expectations and boundaries, including what's non-negotiable.

Inconsistency is the number one killer of boundaries and expectations. My husband and I teamed up to make sure we're consistent about enforcing boundaries and expectations with our children. Believe me, it wasn't like that a few years back.

One rainy night, when our son was almost 6 and our daughter was four, my husband and I were chilling in the living room. The rain suddenly began to pour down quite heavily and loudly. Both children ran downstairs and stood up in front of my husband looking quite scared.

I said, "Why don't you guys come sit next to me?

My son answered: "No, because you're mean. I want to sit next to papa. He's nice."

I was quite hurt and shocked, as you can imagine. I gave my husband 'the look' (I'm sure you know what I'm talking about!) and said: "We need to talk!"

Granted, this happened a few minutes after I had gone upstairs and told both children to not leave their rooms until they finished putting away their toys.

My husband and I had a long conversation about consistency in discipline. See, he's an extremely patient, calm, loving father. My fairy godmother didn't grant me with these gifts. His level of tolerance is significantly higher than mine. So, for a while, I was the main disciplinarian in our home. It took effort and a few conversations, but now we're pretty consistent. He still is calm and patient and I'm still inpatient. Regardless, we're working on it.

Discipline is about teaching proper behavior and changing or modifying undesired behavior so that your child can become a productive, healthy and purposeful member of society. It's also about setting limits and teaching your child to live within those limits.

When, we as parents, provide inconsistent discipline to our children, we're sending mixed messages and confusing our kids. If you tell your child she can use the phone until 9:30 p.m. yet her father lets her stay on the phone until midnight, why would she honor your boundaries? After all, she knows her father will back her up.

Both parents must set boundaries and expectations and enforce them together. I encourage you to sit down with your child's father or partner to have a serious conversation about this matter. If this is a delicate topic in your relationship, be tactful. Introduce it during a time in which your partner is not under stress and start the conversation by expressing your desire to team up and work together for the benefit of your child.

If your child lives between two homes, I know it can be challenging to provide consistent boundaries and expectations. The truth is, you can't control what's allowed or not allowed at her dad's home. But you can certainly control what is and what is not allowed at your home. If your daughter or son is receiving different messages at their dad's, it's important that you have a conversation with them and remain consistent. Be clear about what the boundaries are when they're with you and that you expect them to respect it.

I know this is a complicated situation for you and your tween or teen. However, if you remain consistent and clear as to why you have in place those boundaries and expectations, she will learn to adjust. As she grows up, she will decide what's best for her.

Hang in there. Remember, moms don't quit!

By now, you're probably wondering why I haven't mentioned anything about rules. Well, we don't use the word rules in our home. We set boundaries and have expectations.

When we think about rules, we think about dictatorship—someone telling us what to do without our input or consideration. Consequently, we feel irritated, possibly rebellious and tempted to break them. Rarely, will you meet a tween or teen that says, "I love rules. My goal in life is to follow them."

However, when we use the word expectation, it creates a sense of responsibility and ownership. We're also sending the message, "I know you can handle this!" It's a mind game. I encourage you to use it to your favor.

Wrapping Up

Even when we set boundaries and clear expectations, our children will try to push our buttons and get away with things. That's why it's important to be consistent and clear about what's acceptable and what's not. Most tweens and teens want their parents' approval, especially their moms.

Have a conversation about the reasons behind these boundaries and tell them you know they can handle them. Provide the motivation and encouragement your tween or teen needs to respect boundaries and own the expectations you've set for them. As your tween or teen begins to understand the boundaries and expectations you've set for them, they'll be willing to listen and more open to your guidance.

Teaching and Modeling The Desired behavior

For decades, many parents have relied on spanking, grounding, taking away, or punishment as ways of disciplining their children. Some parents swear by these techniques claiming their children grew up to be healthy adults. Although I'm not here to judge the discipline choices of other parents, I believe we can raise a healthy, confident, independent child without solely relying on punitive discipline.

When I was practicing, I worked with quite a few angry unstable tweens and teens. Curiously, most shared one thing in common—parents used punitive discipline. They were spanked, punished and grounded as they were growing up.

Unfortunately, this form of discipline didn't change or replace undesired behavior. In most situations however, it created hatred, hostility, and resentment toward the parent. These youngsters ended up requiring professional help to cope with school, home, and society.

What I've been noticing throughout the years is that grounding, taking away or punishing doesn't necessarily help your tween or teen measure the magnitude of the offense and its consequences. Neither do they help them regulate and control their emotions, and change the undesired behavior. They do, however, make your child feel miserable and upset temporarily as you deprive them from something they love.

Nonetheless, the undesired behavior is still lingering after the punishment is over. They pay their dues, and depending on how miserable they felt during their punishment, they'll decide whether or not it is worth repeating.

What I've realized, is that discipline at this stage is more about molding your child's behavior. It's about agreeing on and setting appropriate limits for them. I encourage you to set clear limits or expectations and stick to them. I suggest that you involve your child in this process. There are things that are negotiable and there are others that aren't. It's your call. Frankly, they need to believe it's the right thing for them.

Since you're not running a boot camp, keep in mind that life happens and you might have to be flexible at some point. As your child demonstrates responsibility and trust, adjust your boundaries and expectations. Maybe your daughter has demonstrated to you that she can handle curfews. Now that she's 18, consider extending it.

It's important that you stick to your decisions as much as humanly possible. Share your expectations with your child and agree in advance what the possible consequences will be should your expectations not be met. However, don't assume that your tween or teen can handle these limits by herself. Help her behave within the limits you've set and agreed on.

When I was a teenager, back in the glorious 80's, I had quite a few favorite rock and pop bands. But, there was one singer that caught my attention over others—Cyndi Lauper.

A few things I loved about Cyndi were her fearless spirit, fun personality, beautiful smile, simplicity, and most of all—her wild colorful hairstyles.

Oh, my goodness, I loved her hair and wanted to have the Cyndi Lauper look so bad. But, I knew my parents would be pretty upset if I were to shave off a section of my head.

Growing up in a pastor's family added pressures and high expectations to my life. I knew my parents would be upset and perhaps disappointed if I chose to get the wild Cyndi look. So, I didn't bother asking my parents because I knew the answer was going to be a big no.

Regardless of the foreseen consequences, I saved up some cash, ditched my last class and on my way back home, I stopped by a hair salon. I told the hair designer to get me a Cyndi Lauper look. Since there weren't cellular phones back then, I brought a cut off from a magazine to show her exactly what I wanted done in my hair.

I thought, "It's easier to ask for forgiveness than ask for permission."

As you can imagine, I was in heaven when I saw my new haircut—until I got home. I went from being on cloud nine to being grounded for two weeks. Believe me, the pain of being grounded was worth it!

Don't get me wrong. I have wonderful caring parents. Yet, I wish they would've given me the opportunity to have an open conversation about this incident.

As my parents shared with me their position on this matter, I wish I would've been given the chance to express mine and the reason behind my choice. I wish we had taken the time to talk about how I made that decision without consulting them or asking for permission. I wish we talked about what led me to disrespect them.

Did I learn my lesson that day? Nope! Did I feel guilty about my choice? Not at all! Did I rock that haircut? Absolutely! I never got another wild and crazy haircut after this one. But, frankly, it wasn't because I was grounded for two weeks, but because I was no longer interested.

I ask you this, did you have a similar experience growing up? Did your parents use punitive discipline, grounding or taking away? If so, did it make a positive impact in your life? Did you change your behavior as a result of being grounded?

If you've adopted these forms of discipline as a mom, are they giving your child the strategies she needs to not repeat the undesired behavior? Are they helping him see the need and benefits of changing the undesired behavior? If you answer yes to the last two questions, maybe you're heading in the right direction and these forms of discipline might be working for your child. If your answer is no, let's keep talking about it.

When our son turned 13-years old, his soccer team opened a Twitter account to communicate with each other and receive updates about the team's practices and games. Although reluctantly, we allowed him to open a Twitter account so that he could stay in touch with his soccer team.

I told him, "I know you're a responsible child which is why we're agreeing to this. I want you to be very careful about what you post. Keep in mind that once posted, it will always stay on the web."

So, I went over the whole shebang about the dangers of social media. After a week or two, my husband and I called him down to the living room. I asked him to open his Twitter account on his phone so that we could take a look at his tweets. As you can imagine, he was shocked about my request. I found out he re-tweeted a very silly video. As a result, I became upset about his poor choice.

My husband and I were faced with two options. Option one was to delete the account and take his phone away for a while. Maybe ground him for a few days to torture him more. Option two was to discuss the issue and teach the desired behavior.

We chose option two. We talked about the reasons why he shared the video, why it was wrong to share the video, and what our expectations were now that he's aware about our view on that type of content. To earn our trust back, we told him he had to show he's making better choices. We checked his phone more often so that we can go over his tweets. The check-ins began to decrease as he earned back our trust.

We didn't take his phone away nor delete the app because we wanted him to learn how to make good choices and practice self-control. How would he be able to learn these two lessons if we took the phone away or deleted the app?

We reminded him about our expectations and gave him one more chance. He ended up voicing his feelings of regret once he realized how silly it was to share the content he shared. Even today, he tells me how guilty he felt that day and how immature his choice was.

Ironically, he's no longer on Twitter. Maybe you would handle a situation like this differently. And that's okay. The bottom line is we have to help them develop good judgment and teach them to fix their mistakes. Notice I said teach them so they can do it themselves. Don't fix their mistakes for them.

When we take the time to help our tween or teen reflect on how their choice of behavior is unacceptable and the value of making amends, we're teaching them problem-solving skills, discipline, integrity, and healthy moral standards.

> WHEN WE MODEL THE BEHAVIOR, WE WANT TO SEE IN OUR CHILDREN, THEY TAKE IT SERIOUSLY.

The key here is to not only teach your child about self-control and how to make mature choices, but as moms we must also model this type of behavior. When we model the behavior, we want to see in our children, they take it seriously.

A while ago, a mother approached me following one of my parenting talks. She asked me what can she do to help her teen son stop using foul language. "He's always cursing. I wish he would say one sentence without adding the f-word in it."—she added. I shared with her a few tips including modeling the desired behavior. She responded, "Darn it, you're telling me I have to stop swearing as well. That's a long shot!"

You are your child's #1 role model. It's our responsibility to teach and model the behavior we want to see in our children. How can we demand our tween or teen to behave a certain way when we are behaving that way?

Along these lines, we can't assume they already know how to change undesired behaviors. I'm not underestimating the ability of any child. Some youngsters are fully aware about their behaviors and know exactly what needs to be done to change it. However, I'm encouraging you to not assume yours already knows how to change or modify undesired behaviors. Instead, clearly describe the desired behavior, model it, and provide suggestions to help your child succeed.

Say your daughter ignores her curfew and comes home late. Would you choose to yell at her and ground her for one-week or would you have a conversation with her about how she has crossed boundaries and broken your trust? You could then discuss why crossing boundaries is a poor choice and what she's expected to do to earn your trust back? You want her to acknowledge and own her wrongdoing but also develop a desire to stop the undesired behavior. When you accomplish this, you're teaching her values and morals that will take her far in life. Yelling or grounding might not be the best approach for this type of teaching.

Maybe you wake up at 3:00 a.m. and find your 12-years old son playing video games. Will you scold and yell at him angrily, and tell him there's no videogames for one-month? Or, would you consider asking him to turn off the video console, head to bed and discuss the matter the next day when you're less angry?

In the conversation, go over why he's crossing boundaries by playing videogames in the middle of the night (granted he's been told before this behavior isn't acceptable), why he can't repeat this behavior and clearly state what's required of him to earn back your trust.

Unfortunately, if this is your situation, you might have to sporadically set your alarm in the middle of the night to ensure he's no longer getting up to play videogames. If the video console is in your son's room, consider removing it from his room to a common space in the house. Although having screens in children's rooms is an issue that I can certainly spend a lot of time writing about it, to make it simple, consider removing screens in your child's bedroom. All screens should be in a common place in the house.

Wrapping Up

Although spanking, grounding, taking away, or punishment have been used as ways of disciplining children throughout years, I believe that when we have a healthy connection with our tween or teen, clear and open communication and modeling can certainly change or modify undesired behaviors. Next time your child crosses a boundary or disobeys you, try correcting the behavior by discussing the reasons behind his poor choice, help him come up with more appropriate choices, and encourage him to apologize if necessary.

Refrain from fixing their mistakes. It's their responsibility to make amends. At the end of the day, we want our tween or teen to make good choices and practice self-control. As I was browsing the internet one day, I came across this quote: "Don't yell at your kids. Lean in close and whisper instead. It's much scarier." I wish I knew the author!

Fostering a Safe-Zone

If we want to stay connected or re-connect with our tween or teen, we have to foster a safe-zone in which they know they can speak freely without worrying that they'll be punished by default. In her book, *Peaceful Parent, Happy Kids: How to Stop Yelling and Start Connecting*, Dr. Markham suggests that when our child is worried about you getting upset at her, she will move into either a fight, flight, or freeze response as her defense mechanism[12]. In other words, our children can read our emotions and predict our reactions.

If she knows you'll get upset right away without hearing her out first, she isn't going to feel comfortable about sharing personal matters with you. She might even lie to avoid a big argument or punishment. As I've shared in my story about my crazy haircut above, there's always a reason behind our choices. Although it may or may not be a good enough reason for you, in your child's eyes, it's a reason.

As you connect with your tween and teen, keep in mind that you have to create a safe environment so that she can be open to your guidance. Keep in mind that conversations should not only be about poor choices. Sometimes, she may need guidance on how to deal with a personal issue, how to make a wise decision, or how to help a friend in need. Let me share with you six tips to help you foster a safe zone.

1. As I shared with you in chapter 2, it's important to listen. As you begin to listen attentively to your child, she will be more receptive to you and your guidance.

2. Don't interrupt unless it's to clarify something.

3. Remain calm, avoid reacting, judging, or jumping into conclusions instantly. Let them share the incident before you jump to any conclusion.

4. Resist the urge to override your tween or teen's opinion or minimize their point of view. Let them know you're interested in what they have to say.

5. Don't try to control the conversation. Instead, teach your child to identify and explore their options before making a decision.

6. Finally, discuss any consequences and provide choices when appropriate. "Jan, you chose to stay late to watch the show. Now, you're very tired, sleepy and want to go to bed. Yet, you haven't washed the dishes and it's your turn tonight. You can either wash the dishes before heading to bed or wake up 20 minutes earlier to finish your chore before heading to school."

As you seek more intimate conversations with your tween or teen, keep in mind that it may take some time to win their trust and feel safe. When they feel safe to share with you what they've done and you give them the opportunity to express why they did it, you'll be able to brainstorm possibilities to address the issue properly and prevent the undesired behavior in the future.

Of course, there are situations in which an unpleasant consequence will follow as a result of a poor choice. However, the point I am making is that we don't want our children to not share personal or intimate issues with us because they fear us or know we'll make their life miserable as a result of sharing. We want them to know they can count on us, whether to celebrate successes or resolve issues, and that consequences may happen as a result of poor choices.

Wrapping Up

Contrary to popular opinion, your tween or teen isn't indifferent to your involvement. The truth is she wants you to be involved in her life and longs for your support. It's important we foster a safe-zone where our children can speak about their hurdles and mistakes the same way they speak about their successes without worrying that they'll be punished by default.

At the end of the day, you and I want our children to develop internal discipline and healthy morals. We want them to have the ability to make the right choices and do what's right regardless of what their friends are doing. They need our guidance to get there and we need to foster a safe environment that allows for honest, truthful, and difficult conversations between you and your child.

"After all this parenting, I think I'll become a hostage negotiator. Seems less stressful"

—UNKNOWN AUTHOR

4

HELPING YOUR TWEEN/TEEN OVERCOME EMOTIONAL ROLLER COASTERS

*"You don't have to make your children into wonderful people.
You just have to remind them that they are wonderful people.
If you do this consistently from the day they are born they will
believe it easily."*

—WILLIAM MARTIN

As I'm writing this book, our 12-years old daughter is beginning to show the stage one symptoms of what I call the 'Emotional Armageddon Syndrome" or EAS. One minute, she's bombarding me with hugs and kisses, telling me how much she loves me. A split second later, she's upset because I reminded her to wash the dishes.

For crying out loud, we recently finished with our teen son. Can a mom ask for a break?

As children enter the pre-adolescent years, they begin to experience physical, emotional, and social changes. Most parents begin to notice these unpredictable, and, at times, intense mood swings and often find themselves unprepared to deal with these changes properly.

As tweens and teens begin their quest for identity, independence, and deeper relationships, they experience challenges that, if not addressed, may permanently affect their emotional wellness and make the lives of those around them—let's say miserable.

In this chapter, I'm covering three stages of EAS. They are: Stage One: The Mood Swing Spell, Stage Two: Quest for Identity, and Stage Three: Hunger for Deeper Relationships.

I'm also providing some tips to help you guide and support your child during this intense journey so that they learn to face emotional roller coasters in a healthier way.

Does this sound like a plan? Alright, let's get started!

Stage 1. The Mood Swings Spell

Allow me to set the stage for you. Once upon a time, there was a precious princess and prince who loved running around the land's meadows. They were the sweetest, kindest, loving and most respectful twins in the land.

As they were growing up, they were told to never cross over to the enchanted forest. There lived the evil queen who loved to destroy beautiful things. On their 12th birthday, the twins decided to do something special for the occasion. They walked through the meadow and crossed over to the enchanted forest where the evil queen was eagerly waiting for them.

As soon as they crossed over, the evil queen cast a mood swing spell over the twins. She was laughing and celebrating her vengeance against the land's king and queen. Immediately, both children lost their kindness, love, and respect toward their parents—the king and queen. They became vicious beings who felt they can do and say as they please. As days went by, they became more disrespectful and their feelings of entitlement grew stronger. As you can imagine, the family was going through turbulent times and feeling unhappy. The day came when the twins became adults and finally everyone lived happily ever after.

Does this story sound familiar? Is your precious princess or prince becoming a different child now that they're reaching the tween or years? You're not alone! Most kids have a hard time facing their puberty years. They don't know what to do with it. If you remember, our bodies were totally wacked and out of control when we became teens. Between the menstrual cycle, wild hormones, physical development, voice cracking, new desires, and curiosity, puberty can be quite challenging.

Then, you have the teenager who tends to over-react as her world is seemingly crashing down. "I hate school. All my teachers hate me. No one wants to be my friend. Everyone is trashing me on social media. I wish there was no school, ever. My life is a disaster!"

Tweens and teens can be quite dramatic and moody. The good news is that, according to research, mood swings during adolescence are actually normal, aren't necessarily a reason to worry and they shall pass.[13]

I wonder if these researchers have tweens and teens at home? The key here is to help you and your tween/teen manage these swings in a healthier way. After all, we want them to become productive members of society.

Let's go over three tips to help you handle your child's EAS in a healthier way and keep your sanity along the way.

Tip 1. Stay Calm

One thing that worked well for our son and seems to be working well for our daughter is focusing on how we're going to react to her mood swings before we correct his behavior.

As you recall, in previous chapters I talked about the power of modeling the desired behavior over telling kids what to do. What my husband and I have found is that the best way to address our children's mood swings is to remain calm, in control, and exercise patience as we interact with our moody tween or teen.

In other words, don't take it as a personal attack but rather see it as your child struggling with emotional overload and lacking the resources to handle it properly.

Are you surprised? If I get upset and start yelling at my daughter for being moody or disrespectful, guess what she is likely to do? She might feel the need to raise her voice to be heard. On the other hand, if I stay in control and show empathy toward her while addressing the issue, she will likely follow my lead, calm down and feel I care about her. Take it as your opportunity to model the desired behavior.

Tip 2. Play Smart

Most people reason better when they're calm and in a good mood. If you're asking your boss for a salary raise or a higher position in the company, would you do it when she's angry or dealing with a stressful situation? Probably not! The same principle applies to your child. When she or he is talking back at you or giving you a full-blown EAS demonstration, it's usually because she's upset, moody, or simply wants to be left alone.

I'm not suggesting ignoring or pretending the inappropriate behavior never happened. Rather, I recommend that you find the right time to bring up the issue so that they are receptive to your teaching.

When I want to discuss a serious matter with my tween and teen, I usually bring it up when they're calm and receptive to listening. Often times, these conversations happen during a car ride or when they're in their bedrooms chilling and listening to music. I tell them I would like to speak with them for a few minutes and then bring up the issue.

The key here is to avoid coming in with a judgmental attitude or jumping to conclusions without hearing the facts as these two will likely trigger confrontation that may result in an unproductive argument. Guaranteed!

Tip 3. Set Clear Expectations

Most tweens and teens really want to impress their parents and earn their trust and approval. As I've mentioned in chapter three, they love when we are involved in their lives, but also need clear expectations. Have a conversation about how you feel when she respects you and doesn't talk back at you versus when she chooses to do the opposite.

It's okay to let her know that she hurt your feelings and address these emotions, nonetheless, highlighting the desired behavior should be the focus. We don't want our child to develop guilty feelings. Instead, we want them to be respectful and honest. Also, be clear about your expectations. Start with something like this:

> *"Honey, now that you're getting older, we might disagree on a few things. Disagreeing with each other is okay. What's not okay is talking back or disrespecting me when you do. I'm expecting that, when you disagree with me, you'll let me know in a respectful way. Instead of talking back or yelling at me when we disagree, let's have a conversation about it. We can even wait until we're calm to go over it."*

Provide the motivation and encouragement your tween or teen needs to own the expectations you're setting for them. As your child begins to understand the expectations you've set for them, they'll be willing to listen and be more open to your guidance[14].

WRAPPING UP

Raising a healthy child isn't easy. I know, I'm a mom of a tween and teen. We have to keep in mind that we're our children's role models. They imitate what we say and do.

If we raise our voices during a disagreement, they'll likely raise their voices in response. If we lose our cool and control, they'll likely do the same. It takes two to tango just as it takes two to engage in a heated conversation. Next time your tween or teen talks smart at you, I encourage you to take a step back, breathe deeply and do your best to stay calm and in control.

Finally, if your child's mood swings become more intense in late adolescence, it's okay to seek professional help.

Stage 2: Quest for Identity

Identity is more than a first and last name. It's about how we perceive ourselves more than how others perceive us. As your child becomes a tween, they begin to explore their individuality and identity. They realized that the fashion styles and hair-styles mom or dad imposed on them when they were younger, aren't necessarily compatible with who they're becoming. For the first time in their lives, they begin to wonder about who they are, what they care about, and what their interests and passions are.

Let's not underestimate the intensity of this quest. At this age, it's common for your tween or teen to define themselves in relation to others[15]. They not only want to be accepted by their peers but also respected by them. As a result, some teens may go very far in their attempts to be socially accepted. Some experiment with forbidden behaviors (e.g., sex, drugs, alcohol intake), others become rebellious or do whatever it takes to gain that status they feel they deserve even if it's bullying others or hurting themselves. And there's a smaller group of youngsters who are so obsessed with their looks that they are willing to take extreme measures such as plastic surgery or limiting food intake so that they can be accepted.

Some teenagers may even try different identities based on the circumstances or social situation they're facing at the moment. For instance, they may behave one way at home and completely different when they're at school or with their peers.

When I worked for a school system, a mom met with my school team and I to go over the results of her daughter's psycho-educational evaluation. In addition to the team, four of her teachers joined the meeting. Each teacher described her daughter as respectful, responsible, caring, compassionate, and a pleasure to have in class.

"Are you sure you're talking about my daughter?" the mother asked.

On another occasion, a mom shared the following words during a meeting where we were discussing her son's behavior. As she's watching the video in which her son was caught bullying a much younger boy during school recess she said: "What? I don't believe these accusations about my son. I've never heard or seen him hurting other kids, let alone a younger boy. Are you sure that's my son and not some other kid? I'm dumbfounded about the news!" It was clearly her son.

Perhaps your tween or teen is currently riding the emotional rollercoaster and you want them to enjoy the ride. If they aren't yet, don't fret, they'll hop on pretty soon. You'll get your fair share! To give you a head start over other moms who don't have this book, I'm sharing with you two powerful tips you can use to support your child during his quest for identity.

Tip 1. Provide Unconditional Support

As your tween or teen begins her quest for identity, it's important that you're present in their lives, provide guidance and support. It's not about imposing our identity over theirs. Rather, it's about, giving your children the space they need to figure out who they are without the fear of being judged or ridiculed. During this journey, our job is to gently guide and support them along the way.

> YOU DON'T ALWAYS HAVE TO AGREE WITH YOUR CHILD, BUT I ENCOURAGE YOU TO SHOW LOVE, EMPATHY, AND SUPPORT.

This is not a piece of cake kind of deal. Identity requires courage, intense self-reflection, and experimentation. As they go through their identity quest, they'll experience joys, but also pain and disappointment. During these moments, we moms must show our unconditional love and support. They need to know that we are here for them and can count on us regardless of what they're going through. You don't always have to agree with your child, but I encourage you to show love, empathy, and support.

Tip 2. Value Their Uniqueness

When our daughter turned five, she was eager and ready to start Kindergarten. She would ask every day: "Mami (i.e. mom is Spanish), how many days are left before school starts?" See, the thing is, she turned five in June and we had three more months to go. If I didn't do something about this we were up for a long, long summer. To give an end to this madness, I printed a calendar so that she can have a visual countdown and cross out each day until the first day of school.

To her greatest joy, the first day of school finally arrived. She woke up awfully early and put on the clothes she hand-picked the night before. She came downstairs smiling like a sunflower sucking up the sun. My husband and I were having tea and coffee respectively at the table. She stood right in front of us and proudly asked: "How do I look?"

We scanned her from top to bottom. To our surprise, she was wearing mix-matching shoes—same shoes, different colors. So, my husband said to her: "Honey, did you notice you're wearing different shoes? One is black and the other one is silver."

She answered: "Yes, I am. From now on, this is going to be my personal style."

Her personal style? How on earth a five-years old comes up with her personal style on her first day in Kindergarten? My husband and I looked at each other confused.

"Does it bother you? he asked me.

"Not really," I answered.

"If you're ok with it, I'm okay with it," he said.

"I hope we don't hear from the school today!" I added.

And that's how our daughter began her mix-match shoes signature style that she's still rocking today. When she was 7-years old, my youngest sister asked her to be the flower girl for her wedding. As you can imagine, our daughter was beyond thrilled to be her aunt's flower girl until my sister told her: "Sweetie, you know you have to wear matching shoes for my wedding."

You should've seen her face transforming from excitement to disappointment, and finally a big frown. She loves wearing her mix-match shoes and that's one of the many things that makes our daughter unique. The way I see it is this, as long as it's not harmful, inappropriate or against the law, encourage them to explore their uniqueness. Whether it's mix-matching shoes or pink hair, it's okay to let them explore and figure out what makes them unique.

Exploring different appearances in their quest for identify is part of being a tween or teen. Some even replace old interests with new ones. A youngster who played soccer since he was five-years old, suddenly joins the hockey team as a freshman in high school. A softball player decides to join her middle school's dance club and never plays ball again.

Fluctuations in choices and styles can confuse parents but, rest assured, this is normal. At the end of the day, your tween or teen is simply figuring out different identities and what makes them unique[16].

Let me share with you a game plan to help your tween or teen explore and discover her uniqueness. There's no specific order to these three steps, but I encourage you to play smart.

1. Don't panic over changes in appearance or at least try not to show it.
Your son or daughter may (or may not!) eventually come back to their senses when they realize their taste for fashion

is a bit off. And, that unusual hairstyle or color, believe me it'll grow out.

When I was a teen, I became fascinated with wearing black only. My parents became a bit concerned about my new and only color I wore. A few times they asked me: "Are you getting into gothic stuff?" Nowadays, I still wear mostly black because I love it and I don't have to worry about matching outfits. And, no, I've never been into gothic stuff.

Sometimes, we moms tend to make a big deal out of something that isn't the "norm" fearing what other people might say. I encourage you to keep putting your energy on your child and not on what other people have to say.

Tip: Pick your battles, don't make assumptions and keep these issues in perspective.

2. Encourage your child to explore other interests and pursue what resonates with them.

Let me be clear here. I'm not encouraging you to sign your tween or teen up in as many sports or extracurricular events as possible so that they can experience everything before they make a choice. This will contradict what we talked about in chapter two. You wouldn't go to the popular local restaurant and ask samples of every entrée they have on their menu so you can decide what to order? We want to teach them the art of not overbooking themselves and set aside downtime.

Tip: Encourage them to explore new things but stay selective.

3. Encourage your child to identify and write down their qualities and strengths.

There's something about writing things down that make things official. Encourage your child to write a list of their qualities and strengths. Help him with this exercise as we don't want them to minimize who they are.

To some, this may be an easy task, whereas others, may need some encouragement and direction in this area. If you have a child that may be struggling with this task, encourage them to ask their friends and family members for their input. I can picture them saying: "This is awkward!" If this is the case, ensure her it isn't.

Suggest that her closest friend will likely be happy to pinpoint her strengths and qualities. Once they have a few, they can write them on post-it notes or design a nice poster in their computer that can either be printed or uploaded as a background on their devices. Whichever way they choose, they should keep their list of strengths and qualities visible so that they have daily access to it.

Tip: Encourage your child to value her strengths and qualities.

Wrapping Up

At the end of the day, we long to be accepted and respected by others. It's human nature and your child isn't different. He has unique qualities, ideas, strengths, and abilities. Maybe he's still exploring his place in this world or he might not be sure about what makes him unique.

Take the time to encourage and guide him through this process. Pick your battles and avoid assumptions or judgmental comments. It's about how a person feels and perceives herself that counts. We want our children to feel confident and own their uniqueness.

Stage 3. Hunger for Deeper Relationships

I still remember my middle-school friends. We remained friends throughout middle school into high school. We loved hanging out with each other. Oh, how many pranks we planned and executed together! My favorite one was when we came up with the perfect plan to slash the car tire of the meanest and grumpiest teacher in our middle school. We were totally naughty. I agree! The "good" news is that we ended up getting away with it. Side note—make sure your tween or teen doesn't read this particular story. I don't want to give your child ideas and end up being chased down by a mob of angry moms.

I really cared about my friends and loved spending time with them before, during and after school. We didn't have internet access back in the day, let alone social media or texting. We simply hung out and went places together. Their opinions were important to me and so was what they were going through. I wanted to have deep relationships with my friends.

Fast-forward a few decades until today. Nowadays, tweens and teens aren't different. They still love hanging out with each other, value their friend's feedback (sometimes too much!) and long for deep relationships. The difference is that today, technology is getting in their way. Our son and daughter truly value relationships. They're still friends with some kids they bonded with during their elementary years. They appreciate deep connections that come with trust, honesty, and selfless intentions.

Years of experience had taught you and me how a relationship can either be a blessing or a curse. When it comes to our children's safety, we can smell a wolf in sheep's clothing from a distance.

Although we may be able to foresee trouble, our children lack this skill. And most tweens and tees, by default, trust other kids who seem nice. As I worked with tweens and teens and listen to my son and his friends' stories, I hear about teens who have been influenced by peers to give into sex, drugs, and alcohol for the sake of acceptance.

Others share their feelings and personal issues and end up becoming the joke of the school or the top story in social media. It happens more often than not. The reality is, if our sons and daughters lack the necessary social skills to discern who's good, bad and ugly, they're at risk of falling into the cracks and ending up in a fatal situation.

That's why we have to be present in our tween or teen's life. Since their hunger for deeper relationships is so vital in their lives, it's important that we coach them throughout this exciting quest. Let me share with you two tips to help your child learn to choose the right friends.

Tip 1. Teach your child what a true friendship entails.

Talk with your child about the qualities of a true friend. For instance, a true friend will look after you, will not put you down and will not share your personal stuff with others. Encourage him to come up with a list of qualities he wants to see in a friend. He can later use it as an evaluation tool when he begins to doubt about a relationship.

Make sure he understands that a true friendship is a two-way relationship and not a dominant-possessive type of deal. It's not about giving and taking as it is about giving and receiving.

Tip 2. Avoid the urge of 'attacking' friends you aren't excited about.

As moms, we don't want our children to have unhealthy relationships. But sometimes, it happens. If your child has a friend who isn't a good influence in his life, avoid talking bad about or putting this friend down. Your child will likely become defensive and angry at you. As I've shared before, when your child turns on the defensive mode, he will likely not listen to what you've got to say. Before you share with him your opinion about this friend, do your homework thoroughly and provide facts.

Say your tween comes home angry because her friend posted a bad picture of her on social media without asking first. This is not the first time this friend posts pictures of your daughter in social media without asking first. At this moment, she needs empathy from you, not a lecture about how horrible this friend is and how she needs to dissolve this relationship right away.

Wait until your daughter calms down and then bring up the issue. Start the conversation with something like this: "Honey, you're right to be upset with Kelly for posting pictures of you in social media without asking you first. I'd be upset too. I know this isn't the first time she has done something like this and you get hurt. Do you remember that list you created about qualities you want to see in a friend? Do you think Kelly is showing those qualities? Do you think a true friend will hurt you over and over again?"

As you show empathy first, your child will likely listen and follow your advice. Remind her you want what's best for her and want her to have true friends. It's not about quantity as it is about quality. One amazing friend can make a greater impact than ten wishy-washy friends. It might take a while for your child to understand this powerful truth. In the meantime, be there for them.

WRAPPING UP

Building identity doesn't happen overnight. It's a long process that requires patience, empathy, and ongoing guidance from us. Although our tween or teen may seem concerned about what to wear to school tomorrow, who to invite to their next birthday party, or what haircut style or color they should wear next, the truth is they're simply exploring who they are and who they want to become. And, experiencing and sharing all these strong emotions (for better or worse!) is part of their journey.

Let's be intentional about modeling healthier behaviors and choices so that our children learn to overcome the emotional roller coasters that come along with being a pre-teen or teen-ager. If a few gray hairs start popping up here and there along the way, don't fret. A new hair-color is a call away!

"Welcome to being a parent of a teenager. Prepare for a large amount of eye rolling, emotional outbursts, and thoughts of running away. And that's just parents!"

—*SOMEECARDS*

5

HELPING YOUR TWEEN/TEEN FILTER EXTERNAL INFLUENCES AND PRESSURES

"Don't worry that children never listen to you; worry that they are always watching you."

—ROBERT FULHUM

In previous chapters I talked about how most tweens and teens are constantly bombarded by conflicting messages and twisted images of what body image should look like, how they should talk, how "being cool" is defined, and what type of friends they should hang out with if they want to be perceived as popular.

To make matters more complicated for these kids, social media, pop culture and the media often glorify being glued to technology and risky behaviors such as addictions, sex, sexting, pornography, smoking, alcohol use, gaming, and gambling.

With such a massive media attack and false messages being fired at our children left and right, filtering external influences and pressures can be pretty complicated for someone who's been alive for a little over a decade. Since so much confusion is on the rise, moms need to be prepared to provide sound guidance to their tween or teen so that they're able to make right decisions for themselves.

In this chapter, I'm sharing three lessons that will help you address questions like, "What makes a relationship harmful and detrimental? How can my child distinguish between a good and toxic relationship? How should they handle peer pressure? Which influential messages should they take in? How and when should I have 'the talk' with my tween or teen?"

Are you ready to go over these lessons? Me too! Let's get started.

When my daughter was in sixth grade, one of her friends suddenly became hostile toward another friend. Friend A would talk down to friend B and call her names. However, she wouldn't behave like this in front of the other friends. One day after school, friend B, whose been put down by friend A on various occasions, sent a text message to my daughter stating; "I know you don't know, but friend A has been very mean to me lately. Everything started after I went to another girl's house. She's been calling me names, telling mean things about me and posting stories about me in social media."

My daughter was confused as she wasn't aware that friend A was being mean to friend B. She was riding the school bus back home when she received the text. My daughter texted friend B to let her know how sorry she was about this situation.

When my daughter came home, I immediately noticed her sad, yet perplexed face. You know the kind of face I'm talking about. I asked if she was okay and she responded: "Actually, I feel mad and sad at the same time."

She shared with me what happened at school. I asked if she thinks the accusations are true. She said she wasn't sure because she hasn't witnessed any of these behaviors.

First, I thanked her for trusting me and then, we talked about how to handle this situation in a healthy and positive way. I asked her what would she like to do to address this issue and she said; "First, I need to make sure it's true. Tomorrow, I'll see friend A during lunch, I'll talk to her then."

The next day, my daughter talked to friend A during lunch as planned. Without resentment, friend A confessed that it was true and proceeded to share why she was behaving that way toward friend B. My daughter tried to intervene, but friend A was not interested in changing her mind.

My daughter was now facing a dilemma: One friend was bullying another friend. My daughter offered to intervene between the two if friend A was willing to have a conversation with friend B. Friend A refused the offer. My daughter came home very sad. She told me what happened and that friend A wasn't apologizing nor giving in.

A few days and weeks passed and friend A kept up with the same attitude. At that point, my daughter found herself needing to decide whether or not her friendship with friend A should continue.

After another conversation about this issue, she decided to dissolve her friendship with friend A. It wasn't easy but she knew she had to do it. She no longer partnered in class with her or called her. She invested less time and gave less attention to her until the relationship faded away.

When I asked what was her reason for dissolving this long-time friendship, she said: "Friend A has changed and I don't need her negative energy in my life." (Can you tell she's her mother's daughter? LOL!) After a short while, friend A stopped bothering friend B.

Tweens and teens are constantly facing these types of situations. I'm sure you'll agree with me in that friends are very important for your tween or teen. But not every kid makes a great friend. How can you help your child handle peer pressure smartly? By teaching her to filter peer pressure smartly which leads me to lesson 1.

Lesson 1. Teach your Child to Filter Peer and Media Influences Smartly

> IF WE WANT OUR DAUGHTER OR SON TO BE SMART ABOUT FILTERING INFLUENCES AND HANDLING SOCIAL PRESSURES SMARTLY, WE HAVE TO MODEL THIS BEHAVIOR FIRST.

As you recall in previous chapters, I talk about the value of being our children's role models. How confusing would it be if we expect our children to be caring, compassionate, and accepting of others for who they are, yet find ourselves making stereotypical comments? If we want our daughter or son to be smart about filtering influences and handling social pressures smartly, we have to model this behavior first.

Relational Influences

As I was writing this book, I received an email from one of my parenting blog readers. It reads like this:

> *"Dear Dr. Yanina,*
>
> *My daughter has been spending too much time with this mean girl lately. I'm not about judging people, but I've seen how she treats my daughter. I read a few texts from this girl and she's constantly putting my daughter down calling her trashy or chubby. I brought it up to my daughter, and she defends her new friend stating she's just kidding. I don't want my daughter to get hurt. How can I help my daughter find better friends?"*
>
> —A concerned mom

It's not surprising to us that most tweens and teens love spending time with their peers. They long for meaningful relationships. And, this is completely normal. We want them to have fun with other kids their age. Good friendships lead to healthy lifestyles. Friends can help each other stimulate interest in music genres, extracurricular activities, and even academically.

My son really enjoys when he can study for a test or do homework with one of his friends. They often use Facetime or Skype to video call each other to study for a test or work on their homework together. Believe me, when they're in a videoconference, it's not all about studying and working on their homework. I often hear them laughing and having off-topic conversations about the latest sneakers launch, the crazy kid caught picking his nose in the locker room or that kid wearing a knock off pair of Yeezys. The important thing is that they get the work done. Kids thrive when they're with each other granted they choose their friends smartly.

Most moms really care about the quality of friends their children surround themselves with. We want them to be selective and careful about choosing their friends. Although peers can be positive and supportive, some can lead our children down a dangerous path. They can encourage risky behaviors like skipping school, cheating, or stealing to say the least.

According to the American Academy of Child & Adolescent Psychiatry,[17] the majority of teens with substance abuse problems begin using drugs or alcohol as a result of peer pressure. And frankly, often times kids give into peer pressure because they simply want to fit in, be liked by others, and fear to be made fun of or left out.

So, let me share a few tips to help your tween or teen handle peer pressure smartly.

1. Foster open-communication between you and your child so that she welcomes your advice. For a refresher on this topic, I invite you to revisit chapter one.

2. Encourage your child to stay away from those kids that pressure them to do things that seem dangerous or inappropriate.

3. Empower your child to say "no" when they feel others a pressuring them to do something wrong or fishy. Remind them what a true friend is like and that a real friend will not put her down or make her do something she doesn't want to. You're welcome to re-visit the list of friends' qualities your child wrote in chapter four.

4. Teach your child to be smart and selective about whom they consider a friend. The reality is you can't be friends with everyone. I tell my kids they have to show respect and be courteous with other kids but they don't have to be friends with every kid. It's about developing a healthy and strong support system even at their young age.

5. If your child already has a downer in their inner-circle, it's time to let go of this relationship just like my daughter had to do when her friend A was hurting friend B. Here are some steps to help her transition this relationship out.

   a. Encourage your child to talk to this friend and share her concerns.

If the conversation takes place and her friend continues spreading negative energy, suggest to:

   b. Gradually cut down the time and attention she's giving to this person until the relationship fades away.

   c. Remind her that she doesn't have to answer every text or phone call from this person. It's her choice!

I can't stress enough the importance of teaching your tween or teen to be selective about whom they call friend and detoxify their inner-circle. Peers are strong influencers in your child's life. And, generally, they are very close to them. Your child values their opinion and listens carefully to their feedback before making an important decision in their life. They can detoxify their relationships and build a healthier and stronger support system.

Media Influence

In this electronic age, it's easier to access information from all over the world. We are more connected than ever before. Just with a click of a button, we have access to the latest fashion trends from New York, Paris, Milan, or Berlin. With such accessibility in the palm of their hands, tweens and teens from all over the world are constantly tormenting their parents to buy the next 'in' thing—day in, day out.

With advertisements featuring images of flawless bodies, perfect relationships, and unrealistic expectations everywhere they turn, tweens and teens lack direction becoming particularly vulnerable and prone to experiencing issues with self-confidence, identity, relationships, and mental health.

The media has been influencing youth for decades. You see it in television shows, commercials, movies, billboards, and celebrities—the very skinny gal wearing more make up than clothes and the buffed sexy guy showing off his six-pack abs. And, of course, there's the popular mean girl who manipulates everyone around her to get what she wants and the football player who entices as many girls as he can just as if they were trophies.

But, there's one boogieman I didn't have to face when I was a teen. It goes by a few names such as web, internet, or social media. Did you know that tweens spend an average of six hours a day and teens spend an average of nine hours a day consuming media?[18] To top it off, more than sixty-six percent of children between the ages of eight through eighteen own their own cell phone,[19] which makes it easier to access media. Forty-five percent use social media and spend an average of 1:11 hours per day engaging in it[20].

Just like you, I was in shock when I read these statistics. How can this be? How can kids spend more time hooked on their screens than learning in school? Between television, fashion trends, music and social media, the pressure is on.

Before I move on, I want to clarify that media isn't all wicked. Frankly, knowledge is power when it's combined with action. Through the media, youngsters can develop awareness and become knowledgeable of what's happening in the world. We want our children to be socially responsible. Hence, cultural, social, global, and political awareness is also important for their development. It not only inspires them to make a difference, but they also become better citizens and care about issues and injustices happening locally and around the world.

"Okay Dr. Yanina, you've given me plenty of boring stats and information about the dangers of media and how it influences my child. I get it! Let's cut to the chase. Shall we? What can I do to help my child become savvy and make smarter decisions for herself?"

Good question! Let me share with you four suggestions you can use to provide guidance and support to your tween or teen.

1. Have ongoing open conversations about media and its messages with your child. As you have these conversations with your child, encourage her to interpret the messages she's receiving. Take a look at the shows she's watching. How do these shows portray the main characters? What are the messages or themes that keep popping up in the show? Is it gossip, envy, sexuality, aggression, perfect body image, popularity, etc.? Encourage your child to ask herself: "Why do I like these people and

stories? How are they making me feel? What values this person portrays? Do I want to be like this person? Why or why not?"

If it's an ad, ask him how does it make him feel and if he's okay with those feelings. When the moment is right and without a judgmental way, share your take on how these shows or movies are posting twisted and harmful messages that can potentially lead to negative feelings and low self-confidence. Avoid arguments and be receptive to your child's take on this issue.

2. Introduce your child to positive role models through mentoring programs, local community groups, or church. Through our church and our involvement in the art world, we've met a few amazing young adults who live purposeful and healthier lives. Something we do often is invite these individuals over for dinner so that they can share their experiences and have conversations with our children. Our son and daughter really enjoy when we host these dinners and get into pretty deep conversations with these individuals. We set the stage and let conversations flow. They usually share the same advice we've been sharing with them. The difference is that our kids are hearing it from someone else. Regardless, it's good when other people reinforce what you've been telling your kids for ages.

3. Monitor what your child is watching and listening. I know it's impossible to monitor every single show or website your child browses every day. But, you can set clear expectations for what they watch. Keep an eye on what celebrities your child is following and what type of personality or message they're conveying. Find out who's influencing your child and, if they're not positive, start a conversation with them. Again, refrain from

accusatory or judgmental statements. When necessary, ask your child to stop watching certain shows or delete inappropriate music from their play lists. Empower them by letting them know you trust they'll make smart decisions about the music they listen to, what they watch, and whom they follow.

4. Avoid screens in your child's bedroom. For this one, I'm going to spend way more time than I've spent on my first three suggestions. So please bear with me. I promise, it'll be worth it. If your tween or teen has a television, video game console or a computer in her bedroom, I encourage you to rethink this.

When our son was 10-years old, he asked if he could have a television and video game console in his bedroom now that he was old enough. *"All my friends are allowed to have their computer, TV and video game consoles in their bedrooms, can I?"* – he added.

I don't know if all of his friends were allowed to have electronic devices in their rooms, but I do know some of them were. Of course, he was trying to make a statement. Without thinking about it twice, I told him: "No son, screens are not allowed in your bedroom."

As you can imagine, he was pretty upset. I explained my reasons and, although he disagreed with me, he eventually stopped asking. You might be wondering why I don't allow my children to have screens in their bedroom. I'll be happy to share with you four of many reasons why I don't want to take that road with my tween and teen.

Reason #1: Isolation
Youngsters who have screens in their rooms stay in their rooms. They come home from school straight to their bedrooms and lock themselves inside their bedrooms. Why bother coming

out of their bedrooms when they have enough 'access' and entertainment there to keep them busy.

They might come out to use the bathroom once in a while, but mainly, these kids stay in their rooms for hours. Whether they're engaging in online activities with others, browsing the internet or playing video games, they don't see the need to come out of their rooms. Some begin to behave as if they live in an all-inclusive resort at an exotic island in the middle of the Caribbean Sea. They only come out when they smell dinner, and if you don't keep an eye on it, they will even sneak the food into their bedrooms.

The danger of this is that communication between you and your child and between other family members is affected. As a result, the connection between you and your child will begin to weaken, and if you're not careful, it might even disappear. Suddenly, spending time with family is not as important as being in his room chatting with friends and watching videos online.

Reason #2: Uncensored Unlimited Access

We know about the many dangers of the internet. As I've mentioned before, we can't control or monitor what our children browse on the web at all times. We can, however, teach our children what's appropriate and what's harmful. We can also make inappropriate content less accessible. There are a few ways to control what they're exposed to such as parental control software and apps. Consider not having screens in your child's room at all. Instead, only have them in common areas in your home.

In my home, the computer is in our home office and the only television we have that's rarely used is located in the family room. If the screens are in a common area, your children will likely be more careful about what they're browsing and you will be able to keep an eye on what they're doing. This will also help you both monitor the time they spend with their screens so that they don't end up becoming addicted to technology, which leads me to my next reason.

Reason #3: Risk of Addiction

You're probably aware about the many types of addictions linked to screens. One that continues to grow among tweens and teens is gaming. I have parents who've shared with me the sad news that their youngsters have played videogames for some staggering 10 to 15 hours in a day. I'm sure you also know a few.

Rather than engaging in the real world, these kids immerse themselves in the fantasy world of gaming. Some dangers of this addiction are that they often isolate themselves from others, some identify with these fictional characters at a pathological level, ignore more important responsibilities and their academic performance begins to take its toll.

The good news is that we, as parents, can set boundaries and teach our youngster self-control. One way is to set limits for screen usage. Some ideas include letting them use their computer or watch television (or tablets) until 9 p.m. (or any time that fits within your family's lifestyle), play video games after chores and homework are completed for thirty-minutes to one-hour (use a timer), no video games during school evenings, etc. In my home, computers and devices are turned off at 9:30 p.m. unless they're using them for homework.

Each family has their own dynamics, and you know your family best. Most importantly, we are our children's role models. We have to model the behavior we want to see in our children. If we model self-control, they'll learn it!

Reason #4: Sleeping Problems

Once you fall asleep, you're no longer aware of what's happening in your child's room. Are your kids on the screens until late at night? Is she staying late posting in social media? Is he playing video games in the middle of the night? Experts have found that kids between ages six and nineteen who use screen-based media around bedtime lack adequate sleep and are usually more tired in the day than those who don't[21].

One reason is the blue light these devices emit that can interfere with the sleep-inducing melatonin. Another reason is that, as they stay up late, they aren't sleeping enough hours. As a result, they wake up in a bad mood, super tired, and have a hard time concentrating. Don't be surprised if they're constantly moody and struggling in school because they're having a hard time focusing and paying attention in class. They're probably struggling to stay awake.

As for our son, he asked me again once he turned fifteen. My answer remained the same—"No." As you can imagine, he wasn't a happy camper. He threw the "You don't trust me!" card at me. I simply reminded him that, it's not about trust. It's about adopting healthy habits. We went over the points I'm sharing with you in this chapter and surprisingly, he was okay with it. And, of course, our daughter doesn't even bother asking.

Yes, I trust my son. I trust he'll make good choices. I also know he can make mistakes. Regardless, I want both children to understand that this is our home where we have conversations with each other. I want them to stay connected with us and with each other not the fantasy world the web offers. I want them to learn self-control, healthy habits, and respect their bodies. I want them to be conscious and smart about what they allow to enter inside their heads. And, I want them to have control over their screen use instead of being controlled by it!

WRAPPING UP

Sadly, our children are exposed to twisted messages by the media, over and over again: "If you want to be someone you have to be skinny, buffed, pretty, popular, sexy, sexual, and sassy." The list goes on. The more they're exposed to these unhealthy messages without guidance, the more they'll believe and accept them.

Even when I was a teen, I remember being enticed by what the media said was cool and in. From wearing certain brands to following the trends and hairstyles to be accepted by my peers, boy was I fooled. Although the influence is strong, you have the power to influence your children and guide them in the right direction. Teach them to be conscious and smart about what they believe, accept, and internalize. Empower them to make right choices and have conversations about the dangers of allowing the media influence their lifestyle and decision-making. Most importantly, be there for your child and be their role model.

Lesson 2. Teach Your Child Some Good Stress Management Skills

As you recall in chapter one, we went over the value of simplifying your family life so that your child learns to simplify hers and learn to live a less stressful life. I can't stress enough the importance of teaching your child to avoid cluttering their lives and overbooking themselves. Believe me, they will thank you when they develop and enjoy the benefits of this healthy habit.

We also talked about teaching your child to adopt downtime (including no-screen time) so that they can relax, explore, create, innovate, and self-reflect. If you need a refresher about this topic, head over to chapter one to browse it again.

At the end of the day, we want our children to grow up and live a healthier fulfilling life. We also want them to become independent, confident, and caring people. This is certainly my hope for my son and daughter. But, there's a plague that's been spreading around for a while and more tweens and teens are getting infected day after day. They call it 'stress.'

I was reading a research report stating that teens experience stress in ways that are quite similar to adults[22]. Teens are reporting not only comparable levels of stress as adults but also the symptoms that

TEENS ARE REPORTING NOT ONLY COMPARABLE LEVELS OF STRESS AS ADULTS BUT ALSO THE SYMPTOMS THAT COME WITH IT.

come with it. Are you as shocked as I am about these results?

The most common sources of stress reported by teens are school, college acceptance, or deciding what to do after high school, and family's financial issues. When I mentioned these results to some of my son's friends, they concur and also added social issues like drama and peer pressure can also be highly stressful.

We know about how stress can take a toll on our mental and physical health and the last thing we want is for our children to experience these issues at such a young age. These kids are starting their lives and are already showing unhealthy levels of stress. This isn't acceptable! If we don't address this now, our children will be facing a troubled outlook when it comes to their mental health. The truth is the more stress these kids experience in their lives without managing it correctly, the more likely it will affect their personal life, family dynamics, and school performance.

For the next few minutes, I want to focus on stress management. When unmanaged, stress can lead to withdrawal, aggression, anxiety, physical illness, or addictions such as drug and/or alcohol use, and many other unpleasant consequences. That's why it's so important that we teach our children to make healthier choices for themselves. Let me share with you six strategies you can do to help your child develop stress management skills.

1. Welcome a conversation and encourage your child to talk about her stress. Sharing her frustrations with you

or someone else has the potential to ease her mind, body and soul. It's about sharing the load with someone else. Be receptive about your child's needs. Sometimes they'll need a safe outlet, other times someone to listen to them or a word of advice.

2. Help your child calm down by modeling the behavior. Interestingly enough, as I'm writing this chapter, my son comes home from school very upset and frustrated because he failed a test he studied very hard for the night before. As he's telling me about it, I sense his frustration along with his increasingly loud tone of voice. I politely interrupted him and said: "Son, I can understand why you're frustrated, but there's no need to raise your voice. Why don't you stop for a moment, calm down so that we can continue our conversation?" As I was saying this, I was conscious about modeling the appropriate tone of voice. "But. I'm so frustrated!" he said. He then realized what he was doing and lowered his tone of voice.

3. Help your child understand two things: (1) she is responsible for the way she reacts to a stressful situation and (2) although she has no control over other people's words or reactions, she has the power to control herself. We can't prevent some situations from happening, but we can teach our children to control how they react to stressful situations so they don't get the best of them. Encourage them to evaluate the situation by asking themselves these questions:

- Is it worth it to engage in this nasty game, power struggle or argument?

- What will I get from engaging in this situation?

- What are the consequences?

- Should I stick out my chin and grin and say: "It's not worth it!" (I bet you're singing or humming Annie's soundtrack "Tomorrow.")

An all-time example is the school bully. Typically, they feed up from negative attention and seeing their victims get hurt. If your child finds himself in a situation like this, often times, ignoring and walking away can save them a big headache. However, there are some situations in which standing up for himself or herself will prevent a bully from hurting them again. Talk to your child about the value of integrity and how they lower themselves to the aggressor's level when they use profanity or start a fight out of revenge. Although I should point out there's a difference between self-defense and acting out of revenge. Engage your child in conversations about these issues. I tell my children to never insult others, put people down, start an argument or a fight, and always show self-control. However, (and perhaps you might not agree with me on this one) if someone is hitting and hurting them, they have my permission to defend themselves.

4. Encourage your child to adopt a form of relaxation that will help them ease their mind, body, and soul before ongoing frustrations consume their young lives. According to a study by Johns Hopkins University, thirty minutes of daily meditation may improve symptoms of depression, anxiety hence stress[23]. Mediation, yoga and journaling are amazing forms of relaxation. Other alternative healing techniques such as scented oils and massages can do wonders on their bodies. There are so many amazing breathing and meditation apps your child can download to their phones. You can always read their reviews before downloading them. Also do a search in the internet for websites with recorded guided meditations your child can listen to when stressed out and before heading to bed.

5. Teach your child to avoid using negative self-talk. The more your child tells herself these negative comments, the more she will feel hopeless or defeated. If negative self-talk comes naturally to your child, you might have to guide them in this area. When you hear your child saying negative comments, encourage her to challenge them and replace with alternative neutral or positive thoughts. "I'm going to fail school" can be replaced with "I'm upset right now, but school can get better if I keep trying and get some help."

6. Encourage your child to take a break when she's overly stressed. Whether the stress was triggered by studying for a hard test, just had an argument with a friend or failed a test she's been studying for the past week like my son, it's important to take a moment to ground themselves and clear their minds. Encourage them to do something they really like for a few minutes such as drawing, writing on a journal, listening to music, talking to a friend, or spending time with a pet. Once they calm down, they'll likely be able to come up with solutions or a plan to manage the stressful situation more efficiently. I suggest you're very clear from the get-go that this is a break not a half-day retreat or an excuse to avoid doing their chores. You know how it goes when you're not clear. Your words can get "misunderstood!"

WRAPPING UP

Stress is unavoidable. As much as we would love for our children to live a stress-free life, it's impossible. We can, however, teach and model healthy stress management skills so that stress doesn't take control over their lives. Remember, we're our children's greatest role models and they're constantly watching us. It's my hope that these techniques help your child manage his stress in a healthier way. But keep in mind that if your tween or teen tells you or shows that he's overly stressed, consulting with a qualified mental health professional may be the next step. Some tweens and teens simply need consistent individualized support in this area. If this is your child, it's okay to seek help!

Lesson 3. Be Available and Open to Have "The Talk."

I've spoken with a few moms who have difficulty starting or having a conversation about sex, sexual orientation, and pornography with their tweens and teens. I understand how difficult this can be to some moms, especially when we still see them as our babies. I've been asked quite a few times when and how to address this issue in a healthy way.

There's no magic age to begin the conversation about these topics. And, honestly, sexual curiosity begins at a very young age. If you recall, when your child was a toddler, he was likely fascinated about his genitals. As he grew older, maybe he began asking questions about his genitals and became curious about his erections. Maybe, he asked you why his sister's genitals weren't like his. Around that age, you began teaching him about his private area and that no one should ever touch the areas covered by a bathing suit. Right? Needless to say, curiosity continues to grow as they get older.

Now that your child is a tween or teen, there are ways to have "the talk." Let me share with you six tips to get you started. In situations like this one, having a healthy relationship with your child can make a huge difference.

1. Don't wait until your child initiates the conversation or asks questions as they may not know what to ask. Instead, it should be an ongoing conversation between you and your child. As your child turns nine or ten, introduce the basics of puberty and what to expect before they get there. Look for opportunities to go over

these topics so that they feel less intimidated as they approach puberty.

2. As you talk about puberty, let them know that all these changes happening in their bodies (e.g., menstruation, breast growth, acne, wet dreams and body hair are normal. Kids might reach puberty at different ages, but they go through the same changes one way or another.

3. As I shared before, children are exposed to sex and sexual orientation at a very young age. I had a few cases of four and five years-old children who were able to clearly describe a sexual act. Although this isn't the norm, my point is they know more than what we think and we shouldn't underestimate what they already know. Although we have been having an ongoing conversation about puberty and protecting private parts since our kids were younger, my husband and I had the talk with our oldest child the summer before he went into fifth grade, which I confess was quite late. It was a warm sunny day and our daughter was attending a summer camp. As we were finishing our lunch, the right opportunity came up. I wasn't surprised that he already knew a bit about these topics. Regardless, we still talked about sexual intercourse, its consequences and the value of abstinence. We talked about pregnancy, sexually transmitted diseases, and what's used for protection.

With our daughter, just as we did with our son, we began to introduce the basics of puberty when she was about eight-years old. You would think I've learned my lesson about timing when it comes to the talk. Not really. We waited until the summer before sixth grade to have it because we felt she wasn't showing any curiosity. Well, we were late again. She already had some knowledge about sex and sexual identity yet we still proceeded with our conversation. We used photos and educational videos (including information about sexually-transmitted diseases) for both children. Yes, they'll be grossed out, not interested and perhaps embarrassed. Regardless, I believe it's better they hear it from their parents.

4. Sex and pornography isn't the latest news headlines type of conversation. Some youngsters are uncomfortable about going over these sensitive topics, let alone, with their parents. It's important that you don't impose and be okay if they don't want to discuss their sexuality with you at a particular time. Car rides are good for this type of conversations or while passing a couple making out on a park bench. Others are okay with having these conversations in the privacy of their bedrooms. Don't get discouraged. Let them know that you care and that you're available when they're ready. It's safer to hear the facts from you than from the neighbor's 13-years old child who's exposed to magazines and videos through his older siblings.

5. Teach your child strategies to manage sexual pressure by avoiding being in the situation. For instance, my son knows that his room is out of bounds when his girlfriend comes over. He also knows the basement isn't a place for him to hang out with his girlfriend by themselves. Doors are to stay open at all times. Empower your child to set up dating rules such as "no touching of private parts" or "no means no." She can always suggest going out to a restaurant instead of lounging with her boyfriend in the basement without adult supervision.

6. As you have a conversation with your child, don't be afraid to get down to specifics. I encourage you to emphasize sex in the context of relationships, commitment and respect for themselves and their partner instead of disease prevention. Emphasize that sex

should never be forced. Take the opportunity to share your personal values and beliefs about these topics. Most importantly, come to this conversation with a non-judgmental and caring attitude so that you and your child maintain an open and ongoing conversation about these topics.

WRAPPING UP

There's no a magic age or one specific way to talk about these topics with your child. You know your child best and know what works best for her. Needless to say, it's important that you keep an open and non-judgmental attitude so that your child feels comfortable going to you for advice and support. I encourage you to share with them your beliefs about sexuality and pornography. Keep in mind that, at the end of the day, they'll decide for themselves. That's why they ought to be well-informed about the consequences of sexual intercourse and pornography and also how to protect themselves from sexually-transmitted diseases, pregnancy, and addiction.

*"I put my symptoms into WebMD and it turns out
'I just have kids."*

—*SARCASTIC MOM*

6

TEACHING AND PUTTING INTO PRACTICE VALUES, RESPONSIBILITIES AND INDEPENDENCY

"They don't need perfect. They just need you!"

—AUTHOR UNKNOWN

Integrity, values, and character are attributes we esteem and respect in a relationship. Undoubtedly, parents want to raise responsible, independent, and caring adults who live by these attributes. The challenge we face as parents is that, as our children grow older, external influences and peer-pressure become stronger. This is why it's so important that we teach our children positive attributes while providing opportunities that will foster responsibility and independency.

As you teach your child values and pass on your beliefs, keep in mind they'll decide which ones will be adopted and which ones they will let go of. Although I would love my son and daughter to adopt each value and belief we've been teaching them from birth, letting them decide for themselves is crucial for healthy development.

As I've mentioned before in this book, I grew up in a pastor's family. My mother and father were devoted to teaching us integrity and values. They emphasized the importance of loving and caring for others as we care for ourselves. They also passed on many of their personal beliefs to us including the importance of staying connected to God who is the source of life.

As I became an adult, I had to decide which values, views, and beliefs I would choose to adopt. Although I don't necessarily agree with every personal view or belief my parents taught me, I have adopted some as an integral part of my life. Now, I do the same. I'm passing on to my children my values, views, and beliefs. Yet, I am aware that one day they will make their own choices. And, that's okay.

What about you? Did you grow up in a family where values and attributes were taught and expected? Did you grow up in a home in which perhaps values, attributes, and beliefs weren't part of the daily conversation? Whether or not these issues were a part of your upbringing, it's your turn to decide what you would like to pass on to your children. I encourage you to take the time, if you haven't done so yet, to have conversations with your tween or teen about your values, beliefs, and which attributes you would like to see in your child and why.

When I was working at a nearby school system, I had the opportunity to witness children showing love and kindness to others. I saw kids sharing their lunches with a less fortunate classmate or simply because a friend forgot to bring lunch money to school that day. Others were showing their good manners as they said good morning, please, and thank you.

I witnessed a group of seventh graders coming together to stay after school on the last day of school to help their teacher clean up her classroom. I saw teens coming to the local elementary school to tutor little ones for math or science. It was so refreshing to witness selfless children of all ages live their values and attributes while making a difference in the lives of others.

I also witnessed children and youngsters lacking values, sensitivity, and integrity. I saw how little ones easily lied to an adult even though they were caught in the act. I saw others who would talk back to an adult disrespectfully as if they were keeping score. I saw youngsters walking down the hallway insulting, cursing, and flicking their fingers at each other. I witnessed children in first grade showing their peers how to have sex with someone else. I talked to youngsters who felt the need to hurt others so that they could feel good about themselves. I saw how teens disrespected the custodian or lunch lady by yelling: "Hurry up with my food old fart." And the list goes on.

Our society is hurting and there's a need for mending and healing. We need a youth that is caring, compassionate, healthy, selfless, respectful, confident, and shows integrity. They're our future leaders and we need people with values and integrity not only to be in leadership positions but as our neighbors, friends, and co-workers.

Don't you agree?

That's why you and I have the responsibility to do what's necessary to raise our children with character, integrity, values, and convictions so that they become responsible, confident independent adults.

In this chapter, I'm going over three lessons I've been learning as I'm working toward raising independent children with values, convictions, and integrity. I'm also sharing advice and tips you can use as you teach and put into practice values, responsibilities and independency.

Sounds like a plan? Let's dive in together!

Lesson 1. Help Your Child Choose Values and Convictions Based on Truth.

Our youth is bombarded with mixed messages day and night. The media is pretty smart about painting a false picture of how tweens and teens ought to live their lives. They impose their ideas about what's in and what's not, how to act if you want to be popular, even what to watch or believe in. Often times, the messages they are receiving from these unreliable sources are the opposite of what we teach them at home and rarely go in hand with our values and convictions. No wonder why many youngsters are confused about their values and end up feeling at lost.

> MORE THAN EVER, IT'S ESSENTIAL TO STAY CONNECTED WITH YOUR TWEEN OR TEEN SO THAT THEY ARE RECEPTIVE TO YOUR ADVICE AND GUIDANCE.

More than ever, it's essential to stay connected with your tween or teen so that they are receptive to your advice and guidance. I'm sure you'll agree with me in that, you want your child to choose values and convictions based on the truth and not on what the media or the fashion world are imposing. The truth is, we have to build a strong foundation for our tween or teen. And if this is an area that needs improvement in your life, it's never too late.

I'm sure that magnificent buildings like the Burj Khalifa in Dubai with 163 floors or perhaps the 128-story Shanghai Tower in China were not built overnight. It was a step-by-step, brick-by-brick, lengthy, and meticulous process. Just like these stunning buildings took time to be built, it takes time, patience, and consistency to build a strong foundation for our children.

Whether you've already built it or need to start building, it's important that you share with your child your values and convictions, why you're devoted to these beliefs and how are they making a difference in your life along the way. And always model your values and convictions. You can say you believe in many things, but your actions will always speak louder than your words.

We also need to equip our children to thrive and live by their values. Frankly, being aware of one's values is just the first step. What makes a difference is living and making decisions based on our values instead of making decisions to please those around us[24]. As moms, we are here to teach our children this invaluable lesson. As they begin to make their own decisions, they need our help to decide which bricks fit based on their convictions and which need to be discarded. As we assist them in shaping a strong, positive identity, we're also helping them adopt strong convictions and morals based on truth and not on what the media imposes. Here are four ideas to help your child stand up for herself when her values and convictions are threatened.

1. Frequently share your values and convictions with your child, but avoid the temptation of preaching at them.

2. Be consistent about modeling the values you're teaching them so that they respect and trust you. The last thing you want to hear is "But you've never done that before. Why should I?"

3. Have a conversation with your child about her values. Her values may or may not differ from yours and we should show respect regardless. Ask what's important for her, what she values the most and why. Also, talk about what she can do when her values are challenged. Come up with a scenario and plan.

4. Sometimes, tweens and teens need some assurance and a little push. Encourage her to stand firm in her values regardless of what everyone else does or think.

WRAPPING UP

We're surrounded by different kinds of people. There are those who show integrity and compassion and those who are indifferent and only care about themselves. Our world needs more people that live their lives based on integrity, respect, and selfless intentions. We need more people who are compassionate and caring. I know you want your child to grow up to be just like that. You also want her to stand up for herself and be strong. It's our responsibility to build a strong foundation for them and show them through the way we live our lives and present ourselves how a person with integrity and values looks like.

Remember, we're our children's greatest role models.

Lesson 2. Provide Opportunities to Exercise Responsibility

Although each of us has adopted different parenting styles, research has shown that we agree in that teaching responsibility and hard work to our children is highly important[25]. Maybe they might never tell you, but tweens and teens feel good when parents trust and rely on them.

As parents, we can provide our children with opportunities to help them become more responsible and independent. This means, less intervening or fixing from you. For instance, when our children were in elementary school, I would remind them every day after school to give me any forms or notes coming from school staff such as permission slips, announcements, or any important information. Once they started middle school, I told them I would no longer remind them about this because now the expectation is they will be responsible for giving me any school-related communications.

As you can imagine, both children missed out on fun events because they forgot to give me the permission slips. It took each of them one or two slips to finally learn their lesson. I could've signed the permission slip and dropped it off at the school's main office. After all, the school is only a few minutes away and I always enjoy chatting with the ladies at the office. Yet, if I would've done this for them, they wouldn't have learned to be responsible.

Since then, they've learned to turn in important notes and permission slips—often times on the due date (sigh!). Now, we're working on being timely. If we want our children to mature, we have to fight the temptation to fix everything for them. Allowing them to face natural consequences for their lack of responsibility is essential so that they can become responsible and independent youngsters.

This is what a mom who used to be her son's lunch savior had to say about teaching responsibility. *"At the beginning of seventh grade, my son got into the habit of forgetting his lunch at home. Not once but two to three times each week. I have a full-time job, you know. I commute about thirty-minutes every day hence I leave home a few minutes before the school bus picks up my son. During the first week of school, I thought, maybe he's getting used to a new routine. So, I felt bad and drove to his school during my lunch-time each time he forgot his lunch at home. I dropped off lunch for him in the main office and headed back to my office. As you can imagine, I was usually a few minutes late.*

Two weeks passed, and even three. He was still forgetting his lunch at home occasionally. And here I was driving like a mad woman during my lunch to save the day for my son. One day I said: This is pathetic. Enough is enough! It took my son two days without lunch to get it. And actually, I didn't feel bad that he didn't have lunch on those two occasions. He had to learn to be responsible and I was enabling him. I had to learn to stop saving him from the consequences of his bad habits. Now, this kid never forgets his lunch. I'm a happy mom!"

The summer before our son started high school, we went over how he was now fully responsible for getting up on his own. When he was in middle school, he used to get up at 7:00 a.m. In high school he has to get up at 5:20 a.m. to be ready before the school bus picks him up at 6:20 a.m. So, my husband and I were pretty clear that it was his responsibility to wake up and get ready by himself so that he doesn't miss his transportation.

Now, he's a sophomore and has only slept in twice because he didn't hear the alarm. On both occasions, he was late for school. As a result, he had to go to the office to check himself in and got a tardy as a result of not getting up on time. I could've called the school and come up with a good excuse to avoid a tardy on his school records, but I didn't. Now, he's owning this and knows it's his responsibility to get up and be ready so that he doesn't miss his school bus.

We are so used to making decisions for our kids that we have to be conscious and intentional about setting up opportunities for them to make their own choices. As tweens become teens and begin to mature, their view of the world and what's around them begin to expand. They gain new skills and abilities including thinking ahead, alternatives and consequences. They also face more choices and hunger for independence.

As they begin to see the future more objectively, they start thinking about what the future may hold for them. Just because our kids are growing doesn't mean they no longer need our guidance and support. We should never assume that they are fully capable of making responsible choices. Although I agree that some tweens and teens act more mature than their peers, they're still kids. Regardless of your child's maturity level, I encourage you to take the time to teach them how to make responsible decisions[26]. Here are five tips to help your tween or teen own responsibility:

Tip 1. Allow choices. For instance, one of my son's chores is to vacuum the carpet on his bedroom and main level. Unless we have guests over, this chore must be done by 6:00 p.m. on Sundays. It's up to him whether he wants to do it on Friday night, Saturday, or Sunday.

Tip 2. Help your child set goals. Whether it's to get a better grade in Math by the end of the trimester or save some money to purchase the latest pair of jeans, help your child come up with a plan to accomplish her goal. Remind her it's her journey, so she's responsible to work hard to accomplish her goal.

Tip 3. Avoid allowances and let him know you trust him. Keep in mind you're teaching responsibility. There's a time and place for allowances. Certainly, not when the goal is to enforce responsibility. Instead of providing allowances, provide encouragement by letting him know you trust him.

Tip 4. Don't rush to bail your child out when they're being irresponsible. If they make a mistake, let them come up with possible solutions. Position yourself as a guide and not their problem-solver. Be available to provide advice, suggestions, and support. Avoid the urge to give them all the answers and cleaning up their messes.

Tip 5. It's okay to allow natural consequences that result from their poor decisions. Growth will happen when they face the consequences of their mistakes. If they aren't held responsible, they'll keep making the same mistake, won't own their mistakes, feel entitled, and expect you to save them over and over again. They need to learn to own their poor choices and not to blame others. Believe me, getting this straight will avoid major relational problems in the future.

WRAPPING UP

Learning to be responsible and measuring consequences are essential skills for adulthood. We should provide our tween or teen with opportunities so they become more responsible and independent. As hard as it may be sometimes, I encourage you to resist the temptation to bail your child out each time she messes up. It's important that she faces the consequences of her choices so that she learns to make responsible decisions for herself.

Lesson 3. Feed Their Hunger for Independence
When I turned fifteen years old, the first thing I did was to get my driver's license. Oh, how I longed to be fully independent! At least, that's how I saw it. Life became so

amazing the moment that cranky old lady from the Bureau of Motor Vehicles gave me my most precious possession—my driver's license. I was finally an independent woman. So I thought.

Teens thrive to be self-sufficient. They want to be emotionally independent from their parents, make their own choices, and develop their own set of values and beliefs. I know you might not like the fact that your baby's growing up so quickly and becoming autonomous. But, this is normal. At the end of the day, we want to raise independent teenagers that will consequently become independent adults. Let me share four tips to guide your child as they seek independence.

Tip 1. Stay connected and involved in their lives.

Our children need to know we're there for them whether they're a 5-years old child or a 17-years old youngster. One thing I've noticed now that our son is in high school is the lack of parent participation during Parent Orientation Night.

When he was in elementary school, parent participation was outstanding to say the least. Our elementary school had to offer various Parent Orientation Nights because attendance was so huge they were unable to fit all parents in one night. In middle school, I still see a good crowd of parents, but nothing like the elementary school crowd.

This year, during Parent Orientation night at my son's high school, there were a few teacher presentations that had 3-5 parents attending. This is one example of how we can disconnect from our children as they get older. I encourage you to be mindful about staying involved in your child's life. I'm not saying you must attend all Parent Orientations Nights, but make sure you're actively involved in their lives. It's okay to ask them how they're doing in school or if there's a class they're struggling with. Stay connected!

Tip 2. Encourage critical thinking and healthy conversations.

Discuss issues and ideas with your teen and respect their opinion. Encourage them to share their opinions and point of view. At all costs, avoid belittling, judging, or criticizing their comments. Instead, foster a safe environment where both can discuss differences respectfully and come to a conclusion even when both may end up disagreeing. You don't always have to agree with your teen's point of view. However, it's important that you show respect and model the behavior you want your child to demonstrate when he doesn't agree with others.

Tip 3. Teach and provide opportunities to exercise decision-making skills.

Your teen might think she has what it takes to make decisions on her own, but the truth is, she still needs your guidance. Teach her problem-solving skills such as researching for facts, weighing options, and brainstorming possibilities to address issues and situations that aren't going as planned. Also, teach her about the value of identifying pros and cons before making any decision. Keep in mind that your child's brain is still developing until they turn, at least, 21-years old. To their disappointment, they don't know it all even though they're convinced they do!

One thing we do in our home is involving our tween and teen when we make decisions for the family. Of course, there are some decisions that only my husband and I must make, but whenever possible, we involve both children in the decision-making.

What I've been noticing is that, when we do, they feel their opinions are heard and also feel valued. They're learning to own the decisions they make along with the consequences that come as a result of their decision. When we were looking for a church closer to our home, we visited a few churches in the area that my husband and I felt were delivering sound teachings.

You might think my husband and I chose the church we're currently attending, but we didn't. We asked our children to choose the church they would like to attend. We talked about the pros and cons of each church we attended and they decided which church we'll be attending from that moment on. We made sure we exposed them to what we considered sound theology and let them chose the church they felt was the best fit for them not us. This is an example on how you can provide opportunities for your child to be part of family decision-making so that she feels her input is welcome.

Tip 4. Provide opportunities to exercise their independence.

One way to foster independence in your child is by teaching them the value of setting goals for themselves. Start a conversation by identifying what she would like to accomplish in the next week, month, school year, after middle school or high school, etc. Follow it by figuring out together the steps she needs to take to achieve her goals. Some goal examples are making healthier choices for lunch, read three books over the summer, improve or maintain good grades this school year, save money to buy a car during the senior year, maintain a positive mindset, etc.

Other simple ways to foster independence is by assigning chores like doing their own laundry, cleaning their bathroom and bedroom, and washing their dishes. Take them to the grocery store and teach healthy shopping habits. Follow through with cooking skills at home. If I have to mail something in the post office, I usually bring one of my children to do it for me. I wait in the car while they go inside the post office to drop off the mail or package.

Although he isn't driving yet, my son is responsible for putting the gas in our SUV when needed. My point is, provide opportunities for your child to help them become independent and self-sufficient and be okay when they make a mistake. Instead of getting upset and scolding, use the opportunity to correct the mistake. Keep in mind that this is a learning curve.

Another way to exercise independence is by teaching them to manage their money wisely. They need to learn how to do this from you. Take some time to teach your child basic financial skills.

Dave Ramsey, a financial and debt-free expert, coach, author, and host, urges parents to teach their kids about budgeting and long-term savings goals as these are essential skills that lead to creating a vision and developing patience[27].

One thing we've been teaching both children is the value of budgeting and never spending money you don't have. Our son has his checking account and our daughter has her moneybox since she's not old enough to open a bank account. They have their spending money. but also put away money for savings. I encourage you to teach your child how to handle money by opening a bank or investment account once they are old enough so they learn how to manage their money. As a side note, take some time to explain the risks of using credit cards and spending over your budget. We want them to enter adulthood with healthy financial habits. It starts with us.

WRAPPING UP

Most adolescents really want to become independent and responsible individuals. They might not be sure how to get there and that's okay. They have us to guide them through this journey. Be mindful about providing opportunities for them to become independent, stay connected, show patience, and be consistent. In due time, you'll be a proud mama of a confident and independent youngster.

"Behind every great kid is a mom who's pretty sure she's screwing it up."

—UNKNOWN AUTHOR

7

ADOPTING 'ME-TIME' IN MY LIFE

"I hope you know you're capable and brave and significant. Even when it feels like you're not."

—AUTHOR UNKNOWN

Throughout this book, I've been sharing with you tips, ideas, and strategies to help you influence, empower, and stay connected with your tween or teen in such a noisy world. I went over a few tips and ideas to help you develop healthier and stronger connections with your child. I also shared a few strategies to teach, empower, and prepare your tween or teen to succeed.

Now, the focus is on you—your wellness. In the next two chapters, I would like to help you do something that's very powerful, healthy, and essential in motherhood. But, I must warn you, it's something some moms don't see as an option. Depending on where you are in your journey, I would love for you to either begin or keep prioritizing your wellness so that you can live fully and be the best mom you can be.

Yes, I want you to commit to take care of yourself! As moms, we want what's best for our children. From the moment they begin to grow inside our womb, we take on the responsibility to care for, love, and guide this precious gift. In a blink of an eye, they become a priority in our lives. Suddenly, we're willing to give up our next spa day or a desperately needed trip to the hair salon simply because our children's needs are first. We wake up early in the morning and won't go to bed until everyone is tucked in their beds.

There have been countless instances in which I'm at the local chain store and spot that perfect blouse that's calling my name. I listen to the call and walk toward the rack. I grab the blouse, lift it up, look at its front and back. And I look at it again and again, shifting from front to back while trying to convince myself that I'm just trying it on.

I take it to the ladies' fitting room, try it on, and proudly proclaim; "It's a winner!" As I'm taking it off and putting on the one I was originally wearing, I remember that my daughter needs a new pair of shoes and my son needs another box of contact lenses. As I'm walking out of the fitting room, my sense of victory quickly deflates as I spot the rack waiting for my perfect blouse to be left in it.

Am I the only one who tries things on and then that silly little voice in my head reminds me about my children's needs?

REALITY CHECK!

Sometimes, in our effort to become the mom we long to be, we lose ourselves along the way. We numb our needs and when we least expect it, we feel burned out, physically exhausted, and emotionally drained. We run out of energy and wonder why we're feeling this way. Our hair is a mess and frankly we pay less and less attention to our overall health, let alone our looks.

We keep missing our annual exam appointments and forget to schedule our annual mammograms. Does this sound familiar to you? Are you so devoted to caring and raising your children that somehow, you're losing yourself along the way? I'm so glad you're reading this chapter!

Tell me, what happens when a $50,000 shiny red 2-door sports car runs out of gas? Regardless of its cool looks, luxurious interiors or how hot it makes you feel, it's useless! You won't get anywhere without gas in its tank.

Even the most luxurious cruise ship ever built, with its glamorous restaurants, spacious suites, gorgeous interiors, breath-taking balconies, dashing artwork, and exquisite cuisine, it's only just another ship at the port if it lacks its energy source.

> YOU SEE, MOST MOMS WANT TO DO SO MUCH FOR THEIR CHILDREN THAT, SOMETIMES, THEY IGNORE THEIR OWN NEEDS.

You see, most moms want to do so much for their children that, sometimes, they ignore their own needs. Consequently, many end up experiencing physical, psychological, emotional, and relational consequences that can be avoided if we're more proactive and preventive.

Each time I travel in an airplane, prior to taking off, the flight attendants go over a safety demonstration. They cover the items listed on the safety card, share a few inflight announcements and provide demonstrations so that we can be somewhat prepared in case of an emergency landing. When it comes to the air mask, what do they usually tell you to do?

You'd probably hear something along these lines: *"In the event of a decompression, an oxygen mask will automatically appear in front of you. To start the flow of oxygen, pull the mask toward you. Place it firmly over your nose and mouth, secure the elastic band behind your head, and breathe normally. Although you will not see the bag inflate, oxygen is flowing to the mask. If you're traveling with a child or someone who requires assistance, secure your mask on first, and then assist the other person. Keep your mask on until a crew member advises you to remove it."*

There's a reason why you have to put on your mask first before you help your child. If you experience a serious disturbance at a high altitude and you fail to put on your mask first, you run the risk of quickly becoming unconscious from lack of oxygen hence unable to assist your child at all.

This is an example that illustrates the importance of taking care of ourselves so that we are better able to care for our children. As you read this chapter, my goal is to encourage you to take a bold step toward paying close attention to your wellness so you can enjoy physical, emotional, and spiritual strength needed to manage the stressors that come along with being the amazing mom you are.

Before I began to write this book, I interviewed a number of moms to hear their perspective on this topic. I asked each of them the following questions: "*Mothers ought to take care themselves first to better care for their children. What are your thoughts on this statement? Do you take care of yourself?*"

Interestingly, there were two dominant responses among these moms that kept coming up. Quite a few moms felt guilty about taking time for themselves. They said that if they're investing in themselves, they're stealing time from their children. Some added that, they disagree with the statement: "*Mothers ought to take care of themselves first . . .*" Despite their exhaustion and high levels of stress, they would rather focus on their children's needs and ignore or put aside their own wellness.

Other moms felt differently. For them, to be the best mom they can be, they agreed in that they have to pay attention to their physical, emotional, and psychological wellness so they can model for their children a healthier lifestyle.

Among these moms, some said they could rarely fit me-time in their schedules even though they truly believe self-care is essential in their lives. Other moms were intentional about scheduling me-time either on a daily or weekly basis. What I love about this is that those moms who schedule me-time more frequently shared it helps them refuel themselves so that they're better able to meet the needs of their children, be the best mom they can be, and model healthy living. They are clear that it's not about being egocentric or selfish. It's about experiencing a healthier state of mind and clarity so they can make better decisions for themselves and their children.

In the next part of this chapter, I'm sharing two practical ideas to help you prioritize your physical, emotional, and psychological wellness. Frankly, I'm not asking you to spend every weekend at the spa or take a cruise trip to the Bahamas. Although these ideas sound pretty alluring at this moment, the reality is we are busy moms of tweens and teens and can't go to the spa or a cruise trip anytime we want. So, let's go over these practical ideas to refuel your mind, body and soul more frequently.

Idea 1. Experience Daily Joyful Moments

It's just another morning. Picture me sipping my extra hot double espresso latte with no sugar, turning my laptop, opening my emails, and there it was—a venting email from an out-of-state friend.

The email said: *"I'm having a hard time keeping up with everything! Between working full-time on this job that's sucking up my energy (which by the way you know how much I hate it!), family and social responsibilities, I'm totally feeling burned out and stressed out! I'm always crabby and short-tempered. And, I'm not even adding into the equation those days of the month. <<Sigh>> My kids' schedules are taking over my after-work time and I can barely have time to myself. How much longer do I have to juggle all this "crap" around (edited to keep it clean-LOL!)? Way too much to handle /:"*

Have you been feeling like my friend lately? If your answer is yes, you're not alone. It seems to me that more and more people are feeling stressed and over-committed.

So, here's my response to my friend's email—short and sweet. *"Hey friend! I'm sorry to hear you're feeling this way. We moms want to do it all! And, we are constantly juggling too many things at once. Many of us are so busy that we don't even have time for ourselves. We forget to nurture ourselves, especially our mind and soul. At the end of the day, we run out of energy and feel totally burned out. That's why it's so important that we're more intentional about taking care of ourselves. And, a great way to do this is by adding, what I call, joyful daily moments or me-time! As tough as it sounds, the truth is, you have to let go of some things so you can open up space in your busy schedule to have your me-time."*

Let's think about this for a second. What would happen if you're burned out or reach total exhaustion? You'll likely be feeling stressed out, moody, cranky, impatient, drained, or craving for a bottle of whisky.

Well, I'll be the first one to say, you're probably not "hang out" material. And probably, your kids will avoid you at all costs. But in all fairness, how good would it be to have a burned out you around? The last thing I want is for you to end up in the emergency room. God forbid!

TIME TO TWEAK THINGS AROUND

This is why it's so important that you take the time to cool off and nurture your mind, body, and soul. You've got to chill girlfriend! You often hear from medical doctors and the media about the value and benefits of eating healthy and exercising regularly. You know this, and your medical doctor reminds you each time you stop by for your wellness checkup visit. You've got to eat well and rest enough to avoid fatal physical consequences and model healthy behaviors for your children.

THESE DAILY JOYFUL MOMENTS SERVE AS A FUEL TO FILL UP YOUR SOUL.

What about your mind and soul? Are you nurturing these two as well? They're as important as your physical wellness. Just like I shared with my out-of-state friend, I encourage you to intentionally add joyful moments to your day every day to nurture your mind and soul.

Whether it's conversing with your family over dinner, enjoying a glass of your favorite wine while admiring today's sunset, or having some me-time to meditate, do yoga or read a book, it's important that you allow yourself the time to experience moments that revitalize and recharge you. These daily joyful moments serve as a fuel to fill up your soul.

Think about this for a moment. When you feel joyful, doesn't your guard go down? Don't you feel energized, optimistic, and in a better mood? As you experience these empowering feelings, you have more clarity and are better able to make sound decisions.

Whether you're a last-minute person or an obsessive planner, make it a habit to introduce a daily joyful moment to your life. Pursue a spontaneous experience that will take your mind off your hectic busy day for a moment so you can fill up your soul. These mini me-time moments can happen before you head to bed or right after you wake up. Schedule five, ten or twenty-minutes for yourself every day.

When my children were younger, I'd tell them that I needed a time-out. They were confused initially but eventually got it. I printed a stop sign, cut it and added a string to hang it on my bedroom door each time I was in "time-out." I taught them that when the stop sign was hanging on my door, that was my time-out moment.

They cared less at the beginning, but with persistence and patience, they ended up respecting that stop sign. Now that they're older, I don't need to hang a stop sign on my bedroom door. Now they know my me-time routine. I get up in the morning, freshen up and head to the family room's couch to do my devotions and prayer. When my tween heads to school, I head to the gym for an hour before I start my workday. Before heading to bed, I put on my earbuds to do my guided meditation followed by prayer. They know not to interrupt me during my me-time and, most of the time, they respect it.

I can't tell you enough about how much awesomeness these joyful moments add to my life. Between my quiet times and exercising in the mornings, I feel energized and prepare myself to face the day ahead more optimistically. I'm not going to lie to you There are days in which I don't feel like pursuing any joyful moments, and that's okay.

I try my best to care for my wellness as much as I can, so that I have the energy and drive to do what's best for my family. When I'm feeling good, I'm in my best physical, emotional and spiritual mind state. Truly consider making it a habit to experience your joyful moment or me-time not once a week or twice a month but every day!

There's so much your body, mind, and soul can handle at once. Maybe you consider yourself a superwoman. Hey, I get it. I feel the same way too. For as much as we think we're invincible, our energy can last so long before it runs out. But, the epic news is that you don't need to run out of dazzle. Not at all! These small daily experiences are intended to add meaning and rest to your life. When the going gets tough, these joyful moments will get you going!

What can you do in a short period of time that you will truly enjoy? Is it painting, drawing, writing, reading, playing an instrument, writing, yoga, meditation, working out, doing your nails, watching the sunset, or perhaps something else? I encourage you to embrace your daily joyful moment.

Starting today, commit to experiencing, at least, one joyful moment before you crash into bed. Never go to sleep without quenching yourself with joy first. Yes, you deserve to experience joy every day!

WRAPPING UP

Being a mom is very rewarding but it can also be quite stressful and draining. We love our children and want what's best for them even if it means to give up on our wants and needs to meet theirs.

If we don't take time to refuel and rejuvenate ourselves, we'll end up feeling burned out or reach total exhaustion. To be the best moms we can be, it's essential that we take the time to cool off and nurture our mind, body and soul. I encourage you to experience a joyful moment or me-time every day!

Idea 2. Learn to Manage Your Stress. Yes, you can!

Although some stress in your life won't hurt, unmanaged high levels of stress can really take a toll on your health. Stress can affect your physical and psycho-emotional wellness for sure! On the physical side, research has shown that high levels of stress or anxiety can increase the risk of coronary heart disease, high cholesterol, high blood pressure, obesity, gastrointestinal deficiencies, and even premature death[28]. This is serious stuff!

On the psycho-emotional side, people commonly report feeling irritable, angry, nervous, anxious, a lack of interest or motivation, fatigue, feeling overwhelmed, and being depressed or sad[29]. Pretty scary, isn't it?

Although we can't always escape stressful situations, we can certainly learn how to manage stress so it doesn't take away our energy and bliss. Since we all perceive stress differently, it's important that we pay attention to what triggers our stress and adopt strategies to avoid or manage the situation in a healthier way.

Keep in mind that what you consider to be a stressful situation might not necessarily be stressful for other people. And the other way around is also true. If someone tells you: "Why are you so stressed out? What you're going through isn't a big deal!" don't listen to them. Instead, be proactive and learn what you can do to manage your stress. Let me share with you three suggestions to help you manage your stress in a healthier way.

Suggestion 1. Take control of your reactions.

Sometimes stressful situations and relational problems can't be avoided or are out of our control. I understand. Needless to say, because the situation is beyond our control, doesn't mean we can do something about it. You can certainly control your reaction to the situation.

Have you been in a situation where you had a disagreement with someone, whether it's a co-worker, spouse or child, and ended up with a migraine headache, feeling sick to your stomach, and angry for the rest of the day? Or maybe, your son came home late for the second time this week and you simply lost it before he could tell you the reason why he was late was because a cop stopped him for having a burned-out headlight?

We all experience situations like this, and honestly, they're quite stressful. I recommend that, before you spend too much time dwelling on something that someone said or did, take a moment to put the situation in perspective.

During a disagreement or when you're facing a heated conversation with someone, you have to make a split-second decision. You have to decide whether or not this person, whether it's her words or attitude, will dictate your reaction as a result of the unpleasant encounter.

Instead of saying: "You're making me mad!" I encourage you to take ownership of your reaction and think this way: "I'm not going to allow you or your words to dictate my reaction, let alone lose control."

The bottom line is we decide whether or not we're going to allow others to control our reactions and mood state. Since you're your child's role model, keeping your integrity is important. Be conscious about the words you choose to say and the actions you take as they may lead to an unmanageable or fatal outcome.

Say you had a crazy day at work. On your way home, you pick up your son from school and make a quick stop at the grocery store to buy some things you need for dinner tonight. Your son has been whining about going to the grocery store since you picked him up. You're placing the items on the checkout counter and the cashier doesn't even acknowledge your presence.

As she scans the last item, she gives you the total amount due which is $21.50. Yet no eye contact has been established at all. You're tired, really tired. You give her $22. Or, so you thought. She tells you in a sassy, rude way: "Lady, you still owe 50 cents. It's $21.50, not $21.00."

At this moment, you have to decide whether or not the cashier's attitude is going to get on your nerves and ruin the rest of your evening or simply leave the store without allowing this woman to dictate your mood from that moment on.

I know this can be hard sometimes, but, at the end of the day, you have to watch for your wellness and be intentional about what you allow to influence your mood and state of mind.

To sum it up, don't allow others to dictate your mood, state of mind, or how you feel about yourself. The more you control your reaction, the less stress you'll experience. Similarly, the less importance and value you put on people's arrogant comments or reactions, the happier you'll be. My advice to you is be assertive, not aggressive.

Suggestion 2. It's okay to say no.

We all get invitations to commit to different things—whether it's volunteering at your child's school, becoming a board member of a local organization, or coaching your child's sport team, everyone wants your valuable time. And, we haven't even listed your children's extracurricular activities. There aren't enough days to keep up with all the commitments we get ourselves into. It seems to me that "being busy" is an act that's glorified and accepted as the norm in our society. Is it just me? Am I the only one feeling that everyone is so busy these days and they seem to wear it as a badge of honor?

We want to be great moms, productive contributors to society, stay involved, and make a difference. But, boy oh boy, our schedules are so filled up with stuff that not much time is left to refuel ourselves. And frankly, if we're honest with ourselves, half of the stuff filling up our schedules aren't even things we want to do.

We complain that we are extremely busy and have no time to do what we really want to do which leads me to wonder . . .

1. Why do we tend to over-commit?

2. What void are we trying to fill-in?

3. What are we trying to accomplish by overcommitting?

Don't you think that overcommitting is an avoidable and unnecessary stress in your life? The less committed you are, the more time you'll have to do what you love and the less stress you may experience. If you've been infected by the over-commitment bug, it's time to take a good look at your schedule's health status. If you were a medical doctor, would you diagnose your schedule as mild, moderate or severely sick? If your schedule needs some healing, I encourage you to take a moment to answer these questions for each commitment you're involved with.

1. Why did I commit to do this?

2. What am I trying to accomplish by committing to this?

3. How is this commitment contributing to my personal or professional growth or family life?

4. What will happen if I quit it?

5. Is it worth it?

Over-commitments are known for increasing stress, anxiety, and pressure even if you love what you're doing. If you are not careful and selective about the commitments you choose, you will end up feeling burned out and regretting the day you signed up to commit. You will likely come up with pitiful excuses to avoid it.

As these commitments fill up your schedule, there is less and less time available for those who really matter in your life. By default, we are not born to be Lone Rangers. We are designed to be social beings who need each other to live fulfilling lives. Are these commitments worth your isolation from those who truly care about you? Or are you better off letting go of some of the commitments and freeing up space for those who matter to you the most?

As you become selective about your commitments, I encourage you to align them to your personal values and what really matters to you. Not every invitation is the right one for you even if it looks shiny and tempting. If an invitation doesn't match your priorities, you don't need to accept it. Stay focused on what's important for you and your family, not on what others might think or say. When you deviate from your values and goals, you put yourself in a risky predicament. And you'll find yourself regretting your decisions and wishing you didn't accept that invitation.

> STAY FOCUSED ON WHAT'S IMPORTANT FOR YOU AND YOUR FAMILY, NOT ON WHAT OTHERS MIGHT THINK OR SAY.

Be smart, think with your brain and never let the "what would people think about me?" deceitful thought cloud your judgment. Stay focused and say no! The more you say no, the easier it gets. Let me share with you my mantra when it comes to commitments: *"If it's not a heck yes, it's a definite no!"*

Suggestion 3. It's okay to seek professional help.

If your stress is hindering your daily functioning, you ought to pay attention to this matter immediately. Sometimes stress can be overwhelming to the point of debilitating us. And when we are weak, we have a hard time making right decisions and we're more vulnerable to experience severe stress and anxiety that may lead to more serious issues.

If you're struggling about pursuing professional help, I understand. But, I want you to think about this for a moment. If you were getting frequent headaches, you wouldn't think twice about seeing a medical doctor, right? Please don't over-think this. If it's so intense that you might be developing anxiety or other serious issues, I encourage you to not face it alone. Research your options and decide which one is best for you. It's okay to seek help!

Wrapping Up

As you're constantly on the go, be careful not to get caught up in small details. As moms, we don't want to pass on our stress to our children. Believe me, they're very sensitive about our state of mind. They know when we're stressed out. And, unintentionally, we transfer these vibes to them. That's why we need to identify what triggers our stress and learn to manage it before it takes a toll on our health. We want to model for our children a healthier lifestyle but it starts with us. Starting today, commit to a healthier, stress-less lifestyle where you stay in control of your reactions and don't let others dictate how you feel or what you do.

Let's finish this chapter strong. Own these words, "Today, I'm reclaiming myself! I'm no longer allowing others to control my schedule, my reactions, my emotions, or my decisions. It's my choice. I want to be a positive role model and pass on to my children a healthier lifestyle. It starts with me!"

How are you feeling after reciting these words? I'm so proud of you!

"You know your life has changed when . . . going to the grocery store by yourself is a vacation."

—AUTHOR UNKNOWN

8

DETOXIFYING MY LIFE AND LIVING FULLY

"Step out of the history that is holding you back. Step into the new story you are willing to create."

—OPRAH WINFREY

Can you believe we're in chapter 8 already? As they say, time flies when you're having fun! But, we aren't done here yet! We still have some work to do. Now, it's time to reflect on yourself. Overall, how are you feeling about yourself, your life? Are you living fully? Do you have a support system in place? If it's taking you a while to answer these questions, there's a possibility you're in a state of emergency. So, no potty breaks or putting the book aside to read it tomorrow—you've got to finish this chapter today!

There's a reason why we end up being busy moms. We want to do it all. Consequently, we are constantly juggling too many things at once. Chances are your life is pretty cluttered with responsibilities, relationships, and motherhood. If you want to become the woman you long to be, live fully and be the best example you can be for your children, there's one thing you must do.

You've got to detoxify your life. In this chapter, I'm sharing three actions you can take today to start detoxifying relationships, unclutter your life to create some balance, and live a mindful, intentional life.

Does this sound good? Great, let's dive in!

A few years ago, I came to the realization that having a healthy support system or inner-circle is very important. When you surround yourself with authentic, optimistic, and caring people you'll be filled up with positive energy. There's a sense of assurance when you have people in your life you can count on for support and sound advice, get different points of view, and widen your perspective.

The opposite effect is also true. If you surround yourself with negative people, they'll rub on you one way or another. You can fight it, but negativity always finds its way to destroy our souls. Can you say you have a healthy inner-circle? Or, are you struggling with a few toxic relationships that are sucking up your energy and joy? If this is an area you're looking to improve, let me share with you three suggestions to help you detoxify your life and live fully.

Suggestion 1. Detoxify your inner-circle ASAP!

Let's begin by defining what a healthy inner circle looks like. An inner circle is your support system—those individuals you can count on during your great and not-so-great days. These are the people you're comfortable being your true self around without feeling the need to wear any masks. And, of course, these are friends or family members you go to for personal issues and sound advice.

That's why, your inner circle must be healthy to be real. A healthy support system is born out of intentionally developing and nurturing relationships based on trust, honesty, authenticity, and willingness to give without a hidden agenda in mind.

Research[30] has shown that when it comes to being happy, successful, and living a fulfilling life, having healthy relationships is essential. As the old saying goes: "It takes a village . . ." We long to have healthy and authentic connections with other people. It's part of our humanness. Whether you find yourself at the top of your game, enjoying the glory and satisfaction of your success or experiencing challenges and hurdles along the way, having authentic relationships makes our life journey more meaningful.

> CULTIVATING HEALTHY AUTHENTIC RELATIONSHIPS IS PART OF OUR PERSONAL GROWTH.

Personal connections are, by far, essential to our existence. You can have many acquaintances in your life and thousands of friends in social media yet, it only takes one authentic person to brighten your day. Cultivating healthy authentic relationships is part of our personal growth.

There are times in which circumstances make me feel frustrated or disappointed. What I've found is that when I surround myself with those who truly care about me, they infuse me with their love and positive energy I need to keep moving forward.

On the other hand, those who choose to shelter and isolate themselves from others, often times, face the consequences of this unhealthy choice. The more you isolate yourself from others, the lonelier you will feel. This is a dark place to be in and I wouldn't like for you to be there. The bottom line is this, when you become intentional about embracing those who truly care about you, you are building a strong support system based on mutual reciprocity and respect.

Do you have people in your life that raise your blood pressure and make you say things you wouldn't say otherwise just because they're who they are? One way or another, most people get involved with toxic relationships. Toxic relationships can drain your energy, time, and emotional stamina.

I call toxic relationships 'relational vampires.' These vampires mostly call you when they need a favor. They will bring their problems to you expecting you to solve them. And, if you don't solve the problems for them, you're suddenly labeled as not a "real" friend. They show up when they need something. They put you down, make fun of your dreams and bring up your flaws to get on your nerves. They eat your food, drink your wine and when they're done, they magically disappear off the face of the earth until next time.

For your own sake, starting today, detoxify your inner-circle by letting go of the relational vampires in your life! As long as these people stick around, their negative energy will end up influencing you one way or another. Toxic relationships bring unnecessary stress and pain into our lives. And, you really don't need complicated drama in your life. Your kids' drama is more than enough.

Let me demonstrate this for you. Think about someone you know who always sees the glass half-empty, often complains, has an unsteady mood, criticizes everything and everyone and has the gift to make everything complicated.

Do you have a person or two in your mind? Don't you feel tense just by picturing an image of this person in your head? Even though this person is not by you at this moment, just thinking about her or him is influencing your mood in a negative way. This is too much power for one person to have over you and it's not a good thing.

So, my question to you is: Why is this person still in your inner circle? If you have relational vampires in your life, I encourage you to let go of these toxic relationships. If you continue with these relationships, you will likely find yourself exhausted, frustrated, and stressed. However, if you want to live a healthier, joyful, and fulfilling life you ought to let go your relational vampires.

A while ago, my husband Sergio and I took the time to identify our relational vampires. Once we identified them, we removed them from my inner circle. We were able to let go of some relationships overnight, but others required a gradual transition. Yes, it was a very uncomfortable and somewhat awkward process, yet we don't regret any second of it. We made the choice to let go each relationship that consumed our time and energy in a negative selfish way. If we had the guts to do it, you can too!

A healthy support system is not based on convenience or hidden intentions. But you have to take the time to develop these relationships. I'm very selective when it comes to my relationships. I don't want to invest my time, energy, and love in someone who is indifferent or toxic. My time is limited and precious, just like yours. I tend to gravitate toward those who have similar values, beliefs, or interests as mine.

As you surround yourself with amazing people that will lift you up and not put you down, your life becomes more purposeful and worth living. These relationships help us experience the world in a supportive, sincere, and genuine way. They also bring about perspective and clarity into our life. Without healthy and authentic relationships, we find ourselves facing the world alone.

Are you investing in a healthy emotional support system? If your answer is no, let me share with you two tips to get you going as you move toward investing in the right people.

Tip 1. Identify those individuals around you that are toxic and begin the process of elimination.

I understand there are some relational vampires that you just can't let go. Some happen to live with you, others sit on a cubicle next to yours at the office or perhaps others are blood-related. Believe me exposing them to sunlight, silver crosses or using wood stakes hasn't worked for me. But you can, however, set clear boundaries and decide how much time you'll dedicate to the relationship.

If they call you, you don't have to answer every call from them. Whether or not it's a good time to talk on the phone it's irrelevant. Thank God for phone features like silence, mute and voice mail. You don't have to answer their texts unless you think it's necessary. And, you don't have to accept each invitation that comes your way. There's no need to feel guilty about not answering or calling back right away. It's okay!

Tip 2. Identify individuals around you that are authentic and invest in their friendship.

If you want to enjoy the benefits of a healthy inner circle, you've got to work on it. I know as a mom of a tween or teen, the last thing we have time for is mingling or going out with friends. I understand! It's been taking me a few years to select the people for my inner circle. But, at the same time, I'm seeing a pattern.

When it comes to the people in my inner circle, I can tell you that we connected from the moment we met. We didn't become friends overnight, however, there was a spark and positive energy from our first conversation. Honestly, my inner circle is quite small, and it's okay. As I've shared before, quantity doesn't really matter as much as the quality of these relationships.

Cultivate friendships without having a hidden agenda in mind. When you do this, you'll see how relationships evolve organically. I'm not suggesting that you start buying gifts, stalking, chasing people around, or bombarding them with texts. Instead, once in a while, send words of encouragement or support via email or text. Simple messages like: "Wishing you luck or have a great day!" can make relationships thrive. When your schedule allows it, meet at a local coffee shop and let the relationship take its course.

After I detoxified my inner circle, I ended up almost friendless. I'm not kidding you. I had to start making new friends and selectively add them to my inner circle. I can't emphasize enough that it's about quality not quantity. I would rather have an inner circle of three or four authentic, caring, wise, loving friends than a bunch of relational vampires that only bring a false sense of friendship to my life.

The bottom line is good relationships keep us healthier and happier. When you detoxify your inner circle, and invest in a healthy support system you can count on during difficult moments you can develop stress resilience. There is some magic about having a healthy support system that has the potential to ease our mind and soul. Rather than facing your stressors alone, you are able to reach out to your inner circle, share your worries, troubles and experiences with them.

Wrapping Up

Investing time and energy in the right people feels good and it's healthy. By the same token, dissolving toxic relationships in your life feels like someone took a weight off your shoulder. It's simply liberating! There is an amazing feeling of relief when you are able to get things off your chest, learn how others have been able to conquer the same problems you are currently facing without being judged or labeled, and get a variety of perspectives before making an important decision.

There's also a sense of peace when the right words are said to you at the right time. At the end of the day, it's you who decides who will be in your inner circle. I encourage you to be selective and mindful about your relationships.

Suggestion 2. Analyze and filter the source before taking things in.

I don't know if you've experienced this before, but I've met people who **love** giving unsolicited feedback or opinions. There are times in which they are constructive and fruitful, yet other times they can be very destructive and unwelcome. People just love to share their opinions! As you know, my husband and I have a teenager son and a tween daughter. Still, some people keep asking when are we having another child. Good grief!

In my experience, there are people who are *authentic and totally real.* They show care, compassion, honesty and have a legitimate desire to help and see you happy. They love and accept you just the way you're. Some might be in the place you want to be, have walked through your shoes or truly have your best interest in mind.

And, there are those who enjoy sharing their pessimistic and senseless opinions. Some might believe they're helping you, but they're really crushing your soul. Others simply don't have your best interest in mind and could care less whether or not your feelings are hurt. Those who say you're a failure or you'll never be able to raise decent kids! To top it off, you have those who are surrounded by a gray cloud and willingly infuse their negative energy on you. Those who always see the glass half empty and believe there's no hope for this world.

Here you are, getting bombarded with advice and feedback from people and trying to figure out what to do with it. Should I believe Suzy when she tells me over and over again that I shouldn't think about getting a career at this moment in my life? Should I take in my mother-in-law's constant criticism? Am I really not fitted to be a mother like my mom keeps on saying? When it comes to accepting or rejecting the opinions of others, let me give you two tips:

Tip 1. Be selective and choose wisely.
Seek and only consider the advice and opinions of authentic people that truly care about you. Consider the advice of those who have arrived at the place you want to be. They seem to get the big picture and focus on possibilities.

Ask yourself: "Is this woman the mom I want to be?" If the answer is no, perhaps, she's not the best person to give your motherhood advice even if she happens to be your mom or mother-in-law.

Tip 2. Never internalize the words of others without analyzing and filtering the source first.

I encourage you to never accept nor internalize negative and antagonistic words that are delivered to you. Is the feedback coming from a toxic person? Then label it as toxic feedback. Whether or not this person is close to you is irrelevant. Are these toxic words coming from your significant other, parent, co-worker, or a stranger? It really doesn't matter. Label them as toxic and process them as such. Again, there's no need to feel guilt. You have to protect yourself so that you have a healthy mental state to meet the needs of your family.

Keep in mind that your energy is based on your mental, emotional, and physical states. If you're taking in and accepting toxicity in your life, you'll end up poisoning your inner-self and transmitting this negativity to your children. Believe me, they can sense your energy and it can affect them in many ways. Let's explore this together.

Your co-worker tells you you're not fitted for the job and you believe her. You tell yourself: "After all, she's been there longer than I've been." On the way home, you start thinking about what your co-worker said while rehearsing her words over and over in your head. Granted, these words came from your co-worker and not someone with authority.

Nevertheless, you end up doubting yourself and feeling upset. Now your mind is cluttered with negative thoughts and self-doubt. As you walk inside your home, you greet your daughter and the first thing she says is: "What's wrong mom?" She immediately senses that something is wrong. All this happened because you chose to believe your co-worker's words.

Let's think about this for a minute. Is your co-worker in a position of leadership? Possibly no. Is she qualified to evaluate your performance? I doubt it! Does she have your best interest in mind? Maybe, maybe not? Is it worth it to get caught up in this situation and ruin the rest of your evening?

You tell me. Next time, before you internalize a comment, feedback or opinion from anyone, I encourage you to analyze and filter the source first. Don't let others dictate your mood, mind state, or self-worth.

On the other hand, if the feedback or opinions are coming from someone who has demonstrated to care about you and wants to see you grow, or you're finding a pattern where a few people keep telling you the same thing, consider the advice. There are people out there who truly care about you and your well-being. And there are others who really know what they're talking about. At the end of the day, you decide whether or not you want to consider and use their advice. Like some say, it's wise to learn from the mistakes of others!

WRAPPING UP

We all get bombarded with solicited and unsolicited feedback. Sometimes we receive life-changing feedback whereas other times it's worthless comments. Starting today, before you internalize the words of others, first decide if the person has earned your respect, attention, and consideration.

Otherwise, label the feedback as toxic and treat it as such. You wouldn't eat rotten scrambled eggs even if it's served by a world-renowned chef on a fancy silver platter? The same idea applies to comments from others. Be carefully selective about who you choose to be an influencer in your life.

Suggestion 3. Find the balance between family and career that makes sense for you.
One of my clients once told me: "*I want to dedicate more time to my family but I also want to grow professionally. It's getting way too complicated! Between keeping up with the busy schedule*

141

at work, driving my kids to school and all their extracurricular activities, I just don't have enough hours in a day to do this."

Does this sound familiar? We hear over and over about balancing our family and career. But, what on earth does that mean? Are we talking about dedicating 50% of our time to our family and 50% to building our career? Is that possible? Is that realistic? Perhaps your neighbor *Perfect Jenny* can wing it, but, for the rest of us, the 50/50 approach is totally impossible and frankly, unreal!

Let's start by clarifying what I don't mean when I refer to a healthy balance.

I'm not talking about placing your family's circumstances on one side of the scale and your career on the other so they're equally distributed in both sides. The truth is both areas actually intertwine and one affects the other.

Finding a healthy balance is something that only you can define. What looks like a healthy balance for me, might not even be near to what a healthy balance may look like for you. The key is to take time to reflect on and decide where your time, energy, and effort will be invested and be willing to embrace balance as changeable based on the season you're currently living instead of seeing it as a 50/50 cut concept. Since I'm all about sharing tips on this chapter, consider these four tips to help you find your balance between family and work:

Tip 1. Define what's important to you.

Before you conclude that this suggestion is self-centered or egocentric, please hear me out. Most of us have tons of responsibilities and, at times, it feels that there's not enough hours in a day to accomplish everything we need to do. But, if you take some time to outline what you do each day and how much time you allot to each thing you do, you'll realize that often times, we spend time on things that aren't important hence not making a difference in our life or in those around us.

Maybe checking your social media account is taking a lot of time and you don't even realize it. Or, watching back to back episodes of that television show featuring the hot English guy is really enticing you to the point of losing sense of time.

Once you identify what is important to you (e.g., strengthening my relationship with a significant other or my teen, bringing food to the table, moving up in my career, etc.), your actions and decisions

> CHOOSE TO INVEST YOUR TIME, EFFORT, AND ENERGY ON ACCOMPLISHING WHAT'S IMPORTANT TO YOU.

should focus on accomplishing your goals. Choose to invest your time, effort, and energy on accomplishing what's important to you. As a result, you'll begin to value these as assets, experience more balance, and peace of mind.

Tip 2. Press the off button more often.

We are constantly making choices; personal, family, professional, and financial choices. You name it. But, one of the best choices I've ever made is to take care of myself so I can optimize the way I parent my children and be able to make a greater impact in their lives. There are many ways to make healthy choices. Right?

Adopting healthy eating habits and exercising regularly are the most common choices because these two can make a huge impact on your body. Simple good habits can also make a huge difference in our lives. One powerful, yet simple habit is pressing the off button more often. I call it "screen detox."

This involves no browsing social media posts, reading emails, no answering texts, or social media messages for an hour or two each day. I challenge you to do the unthinkable, press the off button more often! It feels great to not hear notifications from social media or websites, texts messages, or email alerts for a few. Often times, these notifications add unnecessary stress to our life. Instead, enjoy a conversation with your tween or teen or call a friend you haven't spoken with for a while.

Nowadays, people are becoming more dependent on their screens whether it's a phone, tablet or emails. A while ago, my husband and I went out for breakfast at a local restaurant. As I've shared before, our rule is to not have any device on the table. The same rule applies when we eat out. Unless it's a business meeting, since we're business partners, we put away our phones in restaurants. Although I admit that sometimes we have to remind each other about this rule when we're out (I'm usually the one reminding!).

As we're waiting for our food, I looked around and saw most people on their phones. Some were texting, others were browsing and a few were playing videogames. Sadly, not many people were actually having a conversation. I thought to myself: What's happening to us? What are we turning into? What happened to personal conversations and human connections?

As we were enjoying our breakfast, my husband and I talked about this new reality and how we have to be intentional about controlling ourselves before it controls us. We talked about a few good habits we can adopt so that screens don't get between us or between us and our children.

For instance, I pledged to silence and not use the phone during my son's soccer games or any of my children's events. I also pledged to be mindful and enjoy these moments without the distraction of electronic devices.

I challenge you to screen detox every day and be mindful so you can also enjoy the moment. Healthy habits keep us in a healthy place. And when we're in a healthy place, we're able to live and pass on to our children a healthy lifestyle.

Tip 3. Be selective.
Just as a reminder, I'd like to start by saying it's okay to say no! If someone told you in the past that saying no is rude, don't believe it! If you're spending time doing things here and there

keeping yourself busy, yet you're neglecting yourself and your loved ones and not living fully, this isn't a healthy balance.

Balancing your family and work isn't easy. Again, it's not a 50/50 cut where 50% goes to investing in your life and family and 50% to accomplishing your professional goals. It's about finding inner-peace with how you're handling and investing your life, embracing that each season in life has its own focus, and what's imperative today might not be as important a few months from now. If you're not focusing on what is important right now, balance is a wishful thinking.

As you begin to see time as an asset you will guard it wisely. This means that, you'll not be saying yes to each invitation you receive from others. You have to be selective! Measure the investment and benefits of each invite or commitment.

What impact will this commitment make in my family's life? Will attending this event make me grow personally and/ or professionally? Will it make a difference in my life or other people's lives? Is it worth it? As you become more selective, you'll begin to differentiate between what's important, what can wait for later, and what's a definite no.

Tip 4. Refine balance based on your current season.

Enjoying balance in your life has to do with the way you invest your time, energy and effort during your current season in life, the impact this investment is making in you and others, and whether you're experiencing the inner peace that comes with doing what's right.

When I was completing my doctorate degree, my son was three-years old and my daughter was a newborn. I was working full-time and had a full load in school. During those years, my priority was to take care of my family as much as I could, work and complete the schoolwork so I could graduate.

My husband was amazing. He really took over everything related to our children so that I could make space in my schedule to do my schoolwork. In my case, I had to cut down the time I spent with my children because I had to focus on completing my degree. For a while, guilt was eating me up. There I was, a mother of a 3-year old and a newborn working full-time and going to school full-time. I didn't have much time to spend with my children. That's when I learned about balance based on life seasons.

You see, my husband and I decided to obtain our highest academic degrees in our professional fields. We took turns and he obtained his MFA in Art first. To do this, we had to make some temporary sacrifices such as spending less time with each other, putting aside family and social gatherings, stepping down from various commitments, and one parent had to take over the needs of the children so the other could focus on school. As you can imagine, there wasn't an equally distributed type of balance in our lives. During that season, each dedicated more time to our education and less time to our family.

During my first year, I felt that my family and career was imbalanced and falling apart. Soon after, I realized there are times in which we have to make temporary sacrifices for the sake of our family's well-being. I accepted this as a temporary season.

After I finished my PhD, I was able to spend more time with my children again. They don't remember much about this season in our family life. But, I learned not to feel guilt when you're making temporary sacrifices for your growth and the well-being of the family. Just be conscious about keeping these imbalances temporarily so that they don't become the norm in your life.

WRAPPING UP

Regardless of where you're in your journey, take the time to identify and embrace what's important to you, invest in your wellness, be selective, prioritize, say no when it's needed, and refine your balance based on your current season. There's no need to feel guilt when your time, energy, and effort have to be focused on a specific goal for a season. Be clear this is a temporary imbalance and you're conscious and proactive about not neglecting the people that matter to you.

"Being a mother is learning about the strengths you didn't know you had . . . and dealing with fears you didn't know existed."

—UNKNOWN AUTHOR

Final Thoughts
Moms Simply Don't Quit.

"Always aim high, work hard, and care deeply about what you believe in. And, when you stumble, keep faith. And, when you're knocked down, get right back up and never listen to anyone who says you can't or shouldn't go on."

—HILLARY CLINTON

Oh, what an amazing journey this has been! Don't you think? You've been challenged, laughed, cried, changed a few habits, and adopted a healthier parenting style. You've been trying different ways to stay connected with your tween or teen and I hope this relationship is getting stronger day by day.

You've come so far and I'm honored to be walking alongside with you during your journey. You've not only discovered many new things about your child and yourself but also affirmed quite a few things you've been doing pretty well. Bravo! You've been so persistent and willing to tweak a few things in your parenting style so you can be a better mom for your children. You've also taken the time to read this book and complete the questions and exercises on the workbook that accompanies it. Well done!

But, you and I know that this journey isn't over yet. There's still plenty to do, maintain, and improve. Keep in mind that pre- and adolescent years are complex. Between the physical, emotional, and social changes our children are experiencing, conflicting external influences and peer pressure, they're in desperate need of our advice and direction.

If our children are going to become confident, independent, honest, happy adults, we must never quit staying connected and involved in their lives so that we can provide the guidance they need during this challenging season of life.

Knowledge without action will not get you far. Start by setting one parenting goal at a time. Focus on one area you want to improve with your child and work toward achieving that goal. Once you achieve it, celebrate together! Next, set another goal and focus on achieving that specific goal. If you set too many goals at a time, you'll likely feel overwhelmed and end up accomplishing a little. Keep in mind that change takes time, energy, and effort.

> FOCUS ON ONE AREA YOU WANT TO IMPROVE WITH YOUR CHILD AND WORK TOWARD ACHIEVING THAT GOAL.

This world is full of noises, pressures, and influences. Despite all these hurdles, you certainly can influence, empower, and stay connected with your child.

Be intentional, consistent, and never give up. Pay attention, be present, and enjoy every moment. Promise me that you're going to take good care of yourself so you can give your best to your family. Most importantly, smile more often, do the happy dance, be kind to yourself, and allow yourself to live fully.

You deserve to be happy! If you're feeling overwhelmed, your worries are uncontrollable, you're experiencing a level of stress that is affecting your daily life, please don't think twice. It's okay to seek professional help.

You know this isn't a goodbye. I would really like to stay in touch with you! I invite you to visit my website at www. DrYaninaGomez.com to learn more about my parenting coaching services and resources designed with you in mind.

While you're there, sign up for parenting and wellness updates that are sent straight to your inbox so you stay informed about future parenting and wellness events. Thank you for taking the time to read my book and I look forward to hearing your story and how this book has affected your parenting style and relationship with your child. Email me at info@DrYaninaGomez.com.

ENDNOTES

CHAPTER 1

1. Harmon, K. (2010). How important is physical contact with your infant? Scientific American. Retrieved from https://www.scientificamerican.com/article/infant-touch/

2. Carroll, J. E., Gruenewald, T.L., Taylor, S. E, Janicki-Deverts, D., Matthews, K. A., & Seeman, T. E. (2013). Childhood abuse, parental warmth, and adult multisystem biological risk in the coronary artery risk development in young adults study. *PNAS, 110* (42), 17149-17153. Retrieved from http://www.pnas.org/content/110/42/17149.abstract

3. Narvaez, D., Wang, L., & Cheng, Y. (2016). The evolved developmental niche in childhood: Relation to adult psychopathology and morality. *Journal Applied Developmental Science, 20* (4), 294-309. Retrieved from http://www.tandfonline.com/doi/full/10.1080/10888691.2015.1128835

4. U.S. Department of Health & Human Services, Office of Adolescent Health (2016). Adolescent mental health disorders. Retrieved from https://www.hhs.gov/ash/oah/adolescent-development/mental-health/mental-health-disorders/index.html#_ftn1.

5. Festini, Sara, B., McDonough, I. A., & Park, D. C., (2016). The Busier the Better: Greater Busyness Is Associated with Better Cognition. *Frontiers in Aging Neuroscience, 17.* Retrieved

from http://journal.frontiersin.org/article/10.3389/fnagi.2016.00098/full.

6. American Psychological Association (2014). Stress in America study. Retrieved from: http://www.apa.org/news/press/releases/stress/2014/stress-report.pdf.

7. Payne, K. J. & Ross, L. A. (2010). *Simplicity parenting: Using the extraordinary power of less to raise calmer, happier, and more secure kids.* New York, NY: Ballantine Books.

8. Common Sense Media (2016). Common Sense report finds tech use is cause of conflict, concern, controversy. Retrieved from: https://www.commonsensemedia.org/about-us/news/press-releases/new-report-finds-teens-feel-addicted-to-their-phones-causing-tension-at.

CHAPTER 2

9 & 10. Simpson, A. R. (2001). **Raising teens: A synthesis of research and a foundation for action.** Cambridge, MA: Harvard School of Public Health. Retrieved from http://hrweb.mit.edu/worklife/raising-teens/pdfs/raising_teens_report.pdf.

11. Merriam-Webster Dictionary found on https://www.merriam-webster.com/.

CHAPTER 3

12. Markham, Laura (2012). *Peaceful parent, happy kids: How to stop yelling and start connecting.* New York, NY: Penguin Group.

CHAPTER 4

13. Nauert, R. (2015). Most Teenage Mood Swings Gradually Stabilize. *Psych Central.* Retrieved from https://psychcentral.com/news/2015/10/16/most-teenage-mood-swings-gradually-stabilize/93561.html

14. Shallcross, L. (2015). Young Teens Suffer Most from Turbulent Mood Swings. *National Public Radio.* Retrieved from http://

www.npr.org/sections/health-shots/2015/10/14/448658923/younger-teens-suffer-most-from-turbulent-mood-swings

15. Bellows, A. (2016). Your Teen's Search for Identity. *Psych Central*. Retrieved from https://psychcentral.com/lib/your-teens-search-for-identity/

16. McNeely, C., & Blanchard, J. (2010). *The teen years explained: A guide to healthy adolescent development.* Baltimore: Center for Adolescent Health, Johns Hopkins Bloomberg School of Public Health. Retrieved on https://www.extension.umn.edu/family/families-with-teens/resources-parents/whats-normal-for-teen-development/identity/

CHAPTER 5

17. American Academy of Child & Adolescent Psychiatry (2012). Peer Pressure. Retrieved from: http://www.aacap.org/aacap/families_and_youth/facts_for_families/FFF-Guide/Peer-Pressure-104.aspx

18 & 20. Common Sense Media (2015). The Common Sense Census: Media used by tweens and teens. Retrieved from: https://www.commonsensemedia.org/sites/default/files/uploads/research/census_executivesummary.pdf

19. da Silva, Julia (2015). Children and electronic media: How much is too much. American Psychological Association. Retrieved from http://www.apa.org/pi/about/newsletter/2015/06/electronic-media.aspx

21. Carter B, Rees P, Hale L, Bhattacharjee D, & Paradkar MS. (2016). Association Between Portable Screen-Based Media Device Access or Use and Sleep Outcomes: A systematic review and meta-analysis. *JAMA Pediatrics.*

22. American Psychological Association (2014). Stress in America study: Are teens adopting adults' stress habits? Retrieved from: http://www.apa.org/news/press/releases/stress/2013/stress-report.pdf

23. John Hopkins Medicine (2014). Meditation for Anxiety and Depression? Retrieved from: http://www.hopkinsmedicine.org/news/media/releases/meditation_for_anxiety_and_depression

CHAPTER 6

24. Weissbourd, R. (2009). Why Teaching Values Isn't Enough: Helping children develop a moral identity. Psychology Today. Retrieved from https://www.psychologytoday.com/blog/the-parents-we-mean-be/200906/why-teaching-values-isnt-enough
25. Parker, K. (2014). Families may differ, but hey share common values on parenting. Pew Research Center. Retrieved from http://www.pewresearch.org/fact-tank/2014/09/18/families-may-differ-but-they-share-common-values-on-parenting/
26. Tiret, Holly (2015). Helping teens learn independence and responsibility: Part 1. Michigan State University Extension. Retrieved from http://msue.anr.msu.edu/news/helping_teens_learn_independence_and_responsibility_part_1
27. Ramsey, D. How to teach teenagers about money. Retrieved from https://www.daveramsey.com/blog/teach-teenagers-about-money.

CHAPTER 7

28. Richardson S, Shaffer J.A., Falzon L, Krupka D, Davidson KW, Edmondson D. (2012, December 12). Meta-analysis of perceived stress and its association with incident coronary heart disease. The American Journal of Cardiology, Vol 110(12). 1711-1716.
29. American Psychological Association (2014). Stress in America study. Retrieved from: http://www.apa.org/news/press/releases/stress/2014/stress-report.pdf.

CHAPTER 8

30. Waldinger, R. (ongoing) Harvard Study of Adult Development (Second Generation). Harvard Medical School. Retrieved from http://www.adultdevelopmentstudy.org

RESOURCES

Moms Don't Quit Mindful Parenting Program*
In this online coaching program, Dr. Yanina offers individualized support to moms interested in implementing more in-depth and personalizing the strategies taught in this book. Dr. Yanina provides guidance and assistance as she helps moms create action plans tailored to their specific needs. She also helps them (1) develop a healthier and stronger connection with their tween/teen and (2) teach, empower and prepare their tween/teen to succeed. These sessions are offered in small groups. For more information, please visit our website at www.DrYaninaGomez.com.

Developing a Healthier and Stronger Connection with my Tween/Teen Talk*
As parents, we want to have strong relationships with our children. We want to be their greatest supporter and influencer. After all, we know what's best for them. As they enter the pre- and adolescent years, some suddenly begin to disconnect from their parents. Mom and dad have within their power the ability to avoid or mend this outcome. To do so, they must develop and maintain healthy relationships with their child by being present, fostering open communication and intentional listening.

In this 90-minute talk, Dr. Yanina shares four powerful strategies to stay connected with your child in a more authentic way. She also shares personal examples and numerous tips and ideas to help parents implement these strategies in a practical way. She concludes her talk by sharing with the audience a few tips to help them prioritize and invest in their personal wellness. To book Dr. Yanina, please email us at info@ DrYaninaGomez.com.

Teaching, Empowering and Preparing my Tween/Teen to Succeed Talk*

More than ever, tweens and teens have easy access to unlimited information with a touch of a button. From hundreds of social media platforms, unlimited easy access to inappropriate content, false and conflicting messages from the media and peer pressure, these youngsters are in desperate need of sound direction and support from their parents.

In this 90-minute talk, Dr. Yanina shares with the attendees strategies to help their youngster navigate and succeed in this challenging developmental stage despite the noises that compete for their attention. She focuses on healthy discipline, helping your child overcome emotional roller coasters, helping your child filter external influences and pressures and teaching and putting into practice values, responsibility and independency. She concludes her talk by sharing with the audience a few tips to help them prioritize and invest in their personal wellness. To book Dr. Yanina, please email us at info@DrYaninaGomez.com.

Boosting My Child's Self-Confidence: Helpful Tips for Parents of School-Age Children*

As parents, we want the best for our children. After all, they mean the world to us! We want to raise confident, successful, independent, compassionate and well-rounded members of society. But, are we unintentionally teaching our child to feel entitled thinking that we are cultivating her/his confidence? In this 60-minute talk, Dr. Yanina shares with parents the Do's and Don'ts of raising a confident child without promoting entitlement or arrogance. Parents will leave with effective strategies they can start implementing right away to help their child thrive in a healthier manner. To book Dr. Yanina, please email us at info@DrYaninaGomez.com.

Moms Don't Quit! Blog: *Parenting Resources for the Busy Mom*

In this blog, Dr. Yanina shares advice to help you address issues in discipline, mood changes, behavior and attitude, social media, and more. She also shares what's working and not working for her kids. And, because she cares about your emotional wellness, she also shares tips and strategies to live a mindful, intentional and purposeful life. Visit our website at www.DrYaninaGomez.com.

Moms Don't Quit! A Facebook Group for the Busy Mom

As busy moms, we've got no time to waste! That's why Dr. Yanina started this Facebook group. A one-stop resource where you'll receive support and advice for moms like you wanting to connect with their tween or teen authentically while keeping up with their busy schedule! To join other moms visit us at: https://www.facebook.com/groups/231807720660651/.

Moms Chat! Podcast

Who said parenting was easy? We all can benefit from sound parenting advice. If you're a busy mom wanting to make a greater impact in your child's life while working toward becoming the mom you long to be, this podcast is for you! In this podcast I chat with moms, just like you, about the joys and challenges of motherhood. I also provide parenting and wellness advice. Find us in iTunes and our website. If you're interested in being a guest in this podcast, send me an email at info@DrYaninaGomez.com.

Moms Don't Quit! Reflective Workbook (PDF)
This workbook was designed to accompany this book. It's available to you at no additional cost. In this workbook, you'll find exercises to help you personalize the tips and strategies taught in this book chapter by chapter. It will also guide you through creating action steps to develop a stronger relationship with your child. The link to download this workbook is www.DrYaninaGomez.com/workbook.

* *Available in English and Spanish*

ABOUT THE AUTHOR

Dr. A. Yanina Gomez is a mindset, emotional wellness and parenting coach, author, speaker and blogger. She has a doctorate degree in Educational Psychology and began her career as a school psychologist helping parents raise their children in a healthier way and working with children from pre-school to high school. She also has a vast experience with various parenting styles, family struggles and providing supportive parenting, academic and behavioral interventions. Her career has evolved throughout the years and among other projects, she helps parents connect, discipline and raise confident, independent and mindful children through her various resources.

As a mindset and emotional wellness expert, Dr. Yanina offers individual coaching, workshops and talks to help women overcome limiting beliefs, fears and lack of confidence that are preventing them from taking a significant step in their life or career and experience greater success. She also facilitates wellness talks for audiences interested in living a healthier, happier and fulfilling life. Her signature topics are stress management, overcoming mindset blocks (e.g., limiting beliefs), strengthening your inner-confidence and adopting a healthier mindset that leads to success.

Dr. Yanina is a wife and a mother of a teen son who plays the piano and trumpet, has been playing soccer since he was five-years old and is working on creating his own urban-inspired online teen clothing store. She also has a tween daughter who began wearing mix-matching shoes at the age of five, plays the violin and alto sax, loves art and has her online store called Awesomesaucenyah at Etsy.com.

CPSIA information can be obtained
at www.ICGtesting.com
Printed in the USA
BVHW042334291121
622797BV00008B/194/J